MANIFESTATIONS
OF THE BLESSING

By:

Dr. Gene Herndon

AiONMULTIMEDIA
"The Word is Eternal" Isaiah 40:8

Printed in the United States of America

Published by Aion Multimedia
20118 N 67th Ave
Suite 300-446
Glendale AZ 85308
www.aionmultimedia.com

ISBN: 9780991565788

Table of Contents

Introduction

Businesspeople face a unique challenge. Oftentimes the very nature of business can cause you to have to blur the lines of your Christian beliefs, if I can say it that way. As a businessperson, you may find yourself in positions where you have to make decisions about how you're going to handle certain things. It's a unique set of challenges that only a businessperson can really understand.

There's also the challenge of trying to run my business like a ministry. I've sensed the gifts and callings of God upon my life and I begin to demonstrate my Christianity (if you will, my faith) in ways that make my business into a ministry. Now, if you have an employee who works for you who can't seem to get it together, you want to counsel them (as opposed to realizing that there is a point where you have to fire somebody and hire someone who can get the job done). The counseling aspect of it is good from a Christian standpoint, but that could take your business into the tank—trying to minister to people who are contractually obligated to provide a service. There are some unique dynamics of that.

Years before I became a practicing Christian, I had experienced some levels of success in business and made some money. I felt pretty good about it. Then when I became a Christian, I began to grapple with whether I was supposed to make money or not. I began to struggle with the question: "Is money good? Is money bad? What's the deal? Do I sit back and see if God wants me to be wealthy and blessed?" I had a lot of legitimate struggle over the years. Then I began to study and develop in my understanding as I really wanted to get the matter clear. I watched these people on TV who said if I give a dollar, that I'll become a millionaire. I had a real problem with that nonsense—and it's still nonsense. Even when I first came into my Christianity, I really struggled with that stuff. I said, "If that's the case, I know a lot of people sent you x amount of dollars, yet they are not blessed. I know those people are not wealthy. I know those people are struggling. Some might be millionaires but I guarantee you most of them aren't."

So I began to wonder throughout the years of trying to understand what this stuff about prosperity is really about. Is everyone going to be wealthy? Is everyone *supposed* to be wealthy? Is there some kind of balance to this?

We get on TV and we're looking for a 65 million dollar jet.

I'll say it this way: I have no desire to speak to what someone else is doing. If God decides to bless them with a jet, so be it. Having been a person who travelled all over this country for corporate America for many years (having to jump off and on planes constantly, checking in baggage, checking out baggage, waiting for delays, things get moved, things get bumped, etc.), I have no problem if God wants to give somebody a private jet. You don't have to go through all these pat-downs, take this off, and do this and do that, touch your toes and cough and all this other stuff. I'm fine with it, I really am. If that gets them home to their family quicker and faster, it's worth it. If the CEO of Coca-Cola who sells sugar water can have one, then I think people who do the eternal business of God are allowed as well. Until you've had to do it, until you've had to be on the road away from your family —well, now you can go home and smooch on your wife. Until you've had to be on the road like that, I don't want to hear anything you have to say.

Here's my question: what's the difference between a 6.5 million dollar plane and a 65 million dollar plane? Are there levels to this? Is there a point where it becomes too much?

That's the thing I'm endeavoring to figure out. I thought the easiest thing would be to take you on the journey with me, and let's see where we end up through the study of the Scriptures. This is going to be something that will build upon itself. I'm going to challenge you to read each chapter of this book so that this can unfold and then we can figure out the answers. We're going to go line upon line and we're going to allow the Scriptures to teach us what God wants us to know.

MANIFESTATIONS OF THE BLESSING

Redeemed from the Curse

Galatians 3:13-14

"Christ has redeemed us from the curse of the law, being made a curse for us; for it is written, 'cursed is everyone that hangeth on a tree; That the blessing of Abraham might come on the Gentiles through Jesus Christ, that we might receive the promise of the Spirit through faith.'"

I would assume (and there are some dangers in assumptions) that there is not one person who is not crystal clear or aware (if you're a believer) that you have been redeemed from the curse. We tend to spend a lot of time making sure that people understand they're redeemed. The curse of the law means that whatever the penalty was for not adhering to the strictness of the law, you have been redeemed from that penalty.

How many of you remember the Charlie Brown Christmas special? One character quotes "Peace on Earth and good will towards men." Peace on Earth and good will towards men is not the peace of God. Many people hear that and they think that means world peace, but it doesn't. There's nowhere that tells us we should experience world peace. I grew up that way, thinking it means world peace. It doesn't mean the peace *of* God, it means peace *with* God. You cannot have the peace *of* God without having peace *with* God. They are two distinctly different things. For me to have the peace of God means I am settled within myself and I can rest in knowing that God is my shield, rock, banner, strong tower; He is my helper, my healer, my victory, my Jehovah Nissi, Jehovah Shalom, and Jehovah Rapha.

By having peace with God on the inside means that whatever anger, disappointment, and wrath God has towards me (for whatever I did or didn't do, for whatever it is my momma and others did) I now have peace with Him and the wrath is now taken away. Good will on Earth and peace *towards* all men means an act of God that says, "I have peace with you. We are not angry with you or upset with you." By *we* I mean the Trinity—the Father, the Son, and the Holy Ghost—three distinct manifestations of one triune God.

Now when I'm redeemed, then I begin to know that I have peace *with* God which ultimately allows me to have the peace *of* God. This is one thing I did not seem to pick up. You know, you can read a scripture over and over again. My spiritual father, Rev. Ricky, said something about this one time that just fired some stuff off in me.

In the church I was raised up, our foundational scripture was Galatians 3:13, so I have seen this no doubt gazillions of times. (*Gazillion* is not an accurate number, but it will convey how many times I have seen this particular verse.) Knowing that we're redeemed was one thing, but then he began to say why we were redeemed. In other words, "So what?" You are redeemed, are you not? So what? For what reason? "So that the blessing of Abraham might come on the Gentiles" (Galatians 3:14).

If you remember, the madman of Gadara had supernatural strength, so much that he could break iron chains and fetters. They couldn't bind him; he ran around all night long in the tombs naked, cutting himself, and other superhuman behavior. That means that when Satan moved upon this madman, he gave him supernatural power. When the madman yielded to Satan, his natural strength increased.

My issue is that many times we think strength is a measure of natural ability. If I want to become stronger, I hit the gym. You go to the gym, you work out, and you build muscle. You have to do things naturally. What you had to do naturally, the madman of Gadara got by yielding to Satan.

I still don't know that you can work out to the point where you can bust through some iron chains. Undoubtedly, all strength and power is really spiritual in nature. If Satan can do it (and he is a mere angel who has been cast down), then my God is able to give supernatural strength.

I don't know if any of you remember the story of the woman whose baby had crawled up underneath of a car on a jack. The jack slipped out and the car fell. The mother literally grabbed that car, lifted it up, and pulled her baby out. How did she have enough strength to lift this car? I believe that God moved. That is what we call a miracle, which is a temporary suspension of natural law. If I go up on a building and I jump off, gravity will kick in, unless God supernaturally suspends natural law which says I will fall and fail. If strength and power can be a work of the spirit, then why do we not understand that prosperity also can be a work of the spirit?

Paul says the reason you were redeemed from the curse is so that you could be blessed. You know how people say, "If you don't tithe, you're cursed, and if you do tithe, you're blessed." Others say, "You know it's not good to say you're cursed." Well, you're not blessed! It's a zero-sum game. To say that I'm not blessed may not mean that I'm cursed like I put a stink-eye on you. To me, to not have God's blessing —if, in fact, my prosperity is a work of the spirit (which is what we're going to endeavor to figure out)—then me working all day, every day is unnecessary.

Some of us have been raised to believe that you just have to work hard all day. "I bring home the bacon!" Here's the problem, the challenge: you end up trading natural things like a healthy life, living long and prospering, not be sickly, and not living long enough to enjoy what it is you broke your neck for. When Paul says we have been redeemed from the curse of the law (and cursed is everything that hangeth on a tree) the reason you have been redeemed is so that the curse comes off of you and the blessing comes on. Which blessing? The blessing of Abraham. Not Abraham's blessing, but the blessing that came *onto* Abraham. He said it might come *on* the Gentiles through Jesus Christ. It is a promise by the spirit.

The blessing that was placed upon Abraham might come upon us through the work of the spirit, accessed through faith. My challenge now becomes if it comes to me through the spirit, then it is a work of the spirit. And if it is indeed a work of the spirit, then nothing that human hands can do can add to it or take from it. Can you increase spiritual things? No, God has to do it; the Holy Ghost has to do it. He supplies the power, God supplies the brains, and Jesus supplies the Word itself. That's how it works. God (the brain) speaks the Word (Jesus), and the Holy Ghost backs Him up with the power. The Holy Ghost is the muscle; He's the bouncer of the club. If you aren't acting right, He shows up.

In order to recognize the *so that*, you have to ask yourself *so what*. You've been redeemed, so that the blessing of Abraham might come upon you by the work of the spirit that you access by faith. Why were you redeemed? Why did Christ give His life for you? So that the blessing of Abraham can come upon you. Cursed is everyone that hangeth on the tree, or the wood, the stake. Who stood on that cross for you and why? So that the blessing of Abraham can come upon you.

Matthew, Mark, Luke, and John are historical scriptures that help you understand historically what has occurred in the Gospels. When you get out of these four books and get into the Epistles, you learn why Jesus did what He did. Every time you interpret a historical scripture, you need to interpret it in light of its application. Yes, Christ died on the cross. We still don't know why the Epistles tell us. The reason *why* He hung on a tree is so that the blessing of Abraham might come upon the Gentiles and the reason He specified the Gentiles was because the blessing of Abraham was already on the Jews. This is why in scriptures one may not be a Jew outwardly, but he can be one inwardly. As a Gentile, an unbeliever, when you believe in Christ you are brought into the household of faith. You become a joint heir and spiritually become a brother and sister to all Jews. You experience the same blessing, the same promises. That's why we are called a Judeo-Christian faith system.

So, the reason you were redeemed, the "so what" is "so that" the blessing of Abraham can come upon you.

I have read this gazillions of times. You always rally around, "I've been redeemed from the curse of the law; I have peace with God and it's great!" But then there's a point where it comes to the forefront of your mind, "Okay, now what?" I've watched many people in their relationship with God get to a place where they say, "Now what?" It happens to every believer. They're living and thinking, "I just have peace with God and this is wonderful and God loves me!" Then all of a sudden, there's a nagging on the inside of them that says there has to be more; there has to be something else. It is *so what?* The answer to the *so what?* is *so that.*

Now, in order for me to correctly understand this, I now have to figure out what is the blessing of Abraham. Once I figure that out, now I can tell what I'm working with.

Genesis 14:15-23 (AMPC)
"He divided his forces against them by night, he and his servants, and attacked and routed them, and pursued them as far as Hobah, which is north of Damascus. And he brought back all the goods and also brought back his kinsman Lot and his possessions, the women also and the people. After his [Abram's] return from the defeat and slaying of Chedorlaomer and the kings who were with him, the king of Sodom went out to meet him at the Valley of Shaveh, that is, the King's Valley. Melchizedek king of Salem [later

called Jerusalem] brought out bread and wine [for their nourishment]; he was the priest of God Most High, And he blessed him and said, Blessed (favored with blessings, made blissful, joyful) be Abram by God Most High, Possessor and Maker of heaven and earth, And blessed, praised, and glorified be God Most High, Who has given your foes into your hand! And [Abram] gave him a tenth of all [he had taken]. And the king of Sodom said to Abram, Give me the persons and keep the goods for yourself. But Abram said to the king of Sodom, I have lifted up my hand and sworn to the Lord, God Most High, the Possessor and Maker of heaven and earth, That I would not take a thread or a shoelace or anything that is yours, lest you should say, I have made Abram rich."

Lot and his wife were a mess. Lot made it out but, unfortunately, his wife did not. First of all, God told Lot to get into the land of Canaan. Abram's father was supposed to go to that land but instead he landed in a place called Haran and he stayed there.

There are things God needs you to do and you can't stop halfway. Just because it feels good doesn't mean it is good. You may have been going at this thing, then you're tempted to give up and you haven't even gotten close to the other side. Don't stop where you feel comfortable because then your children will have to pick up the challenge.

Here's Abram. God told him, "Get up out of your kinsman and go ahead on to a land I'll show you." He didn't even tell him where to go (He'd have lost half of you right then and there). "I'll pray and fast until He reveals where I'm going!" You'll be praying and fasting for the rest of your life. Sometimes, the things God will tell you to do, you may not have all the information you demand with your control freak self. How do I get the honor to call you a control freak? "Hi, my name is Gene, and I used to be a control freak." God put me through a one-step program. He said it's one step, "His way," and it's been one way ever since.

He said to Abram, "I need you to get up and go to a place that I'll show you." In other words, as you go, He'll show you the destination. You truly would still be waiting, fasting and praying, and being super spiritual, waiting for Him to reveal where you're supposed to go when He just told you go. He just told you to do, serve, get involved, support, and give.

This passage says that Abram takes Lot with him. Lot wasn't supposed to go; he's just a passenger. He's just a barnacle.

A barnacle attaches itself to the bottom of the boat. When you bring your boat up out of the water, you're supposed to spray it down so you don't have anything attached to it. You can take one sea creature to another lake by moving your boat from one lake to the next because the creature attaches to the bottom of the boat. Too many barnacles will slow your boat down. A barnacle is not to be confused with what is called a remora, which is a certain type of fish. If you've ever seen a shark swimming in its natural habitat, you will see little fish swimming right beside it, almost attached to it. They work with the shark. Their relationship is symbiotic with both of them benefiting. As a shark eats food, food falls out of its mouth and it attaches itself to the shark's skin. If it is not disposed of, it becomes infected and could potentially kill the shark. Enter the remora, which comes in and eats the food that comes out of the mouth of the shark to keep the shark's skin silky and smooth. They need each other and they have a purpose together.

Lot served absolutely no purpose; he's not a remora, he's a barnacle.

Now Abraham and Lot get to a place where Lot's men are fighting with Abraham's men. Abraham comes in and says, "All right Lot, listen. Your people are fighting with my people and this isn't going to work. I understand I'm blessed, and I also know that what will steal my blessing is strife. We can't have this fighting. We are family, kinfolk. I love you, but you have to go."

Many of you may struggle with your own families because you think, "Well, I'm family and I have to put up with that." No, you don't, but that's another message. Abraham says, "Lot, this is what I'll do with you. I don't care which way you go. You go that way, I'll go the other way. If you choose that way, I'll choose this way." The Bible says Lot chose for himself. He looked around and said, "I'm going to take the best land, sheep, and livestock, and leave Abraham with what's left." Abraham responded with, "My peace is worth more than what you think you can take from me."

Some of you are in situations where people are trying to take stuff from you, and because you don't understand how to avoid strife, they are baiting you into a fight. While they're trying to steal your natural stuff on the surface, they are robbing you blind spiritually under the surface. At some point in time you have to learn if they want your cloak, give it to them. Abram said, "The blessing is on me."

The blessing is not on my car, it's not on my stuff. You hear people say things like, "Oh wow, so-and-so just got a new car! That's such a blessing." No, it isn't; it's a manifestation of the blessing. What blessing? The blessing of Abraham, the one that came upon the Gentiles.

So, Lot chooses and Abraham says, "I'll go that way and you go the other way. That's fine, whatever you want to do. Take the best, take it all; you can have it. Once I get to my place, my God is well able to do exceedingly, abundantly more than I can ask or think. I can walk into a barren situation and when I show up, God will show up." The blessing was not on Lot; it was on Abraham.

If I was Lot, here's what I would have done: Abraham comes to me and says, "Pastor Gene, listen. Some of your people who work with you, they're wiling out. We can't have this. You need you to do something." I'll pull them aside and say, "Listen, don't ya'll mess this up for me. I will cut ya'll!" Then I come back to Abraham and say, "Listen, Abraham! I had a discussion with them, and they ain't going to do that no quiero, no mas. So, we good? Okay, thank you."

Now Lot is in a pickle as Abraham took 318 of his servants born in his house. How many servants did you have born in your house? He had 318 servants, his own army. Lot's in trouble. He went around the house, grabbed the maids and butlers, and said, "Let's go handle some things." You have to be anointed to take the maids and the butlers, go do some battle, come back with somebody, and say, "We sent an army into flight." The sign of being anointing is the fact you can do more with less!

Abraham didn't say, "Let's go get some warriors." He said, "Come on, let's go. Let's go get Lot." I love him, but he's trippin'. He should have never left. I wouldn't have to go get you. It's interesting how he goes, sets these armies into flight, comes back with Lot and all his stuff, then he sees Melchizedek, the king of Salem, or Shalom, which is Jerusalem. Melchizedek is the high priest and gives Abraham bread and wine. As the high priest, he then serves Abram communion and establishes that he is, in fact, the high priest of God.

A teaching exists today that talks about how the tithe is the Levitical priesthood; it's under the law. Therefore, the tithe is not for today because we are not under the law. Here's the problem: Abram is the great-great-great-great grandfather of Levi, which means that the Levitical law wasn't close to being in place at the time of Abraham. By faith he brought his tithe to the one who brought him communion, saying, "I would not take a thread or a shoelace or anything that is yours." He didn't say, "Anything I have I'm going to give you."

Abram went to war. As he's coming back from war with all the spoils, he runs into Melchizedek who is the high priest, and also the king and priest, which was not a common combination. But this is what you see in the New Testament—King of kings, Lord of lords; you are a king and priest.

As he's coming back from war bringing all the spoils, he runs into the king and priest who says, "You know what? Don't worry about it. Just give me this and you keep that."

Abram says, "I will not touch anything that is yours." Who went to war? Abram. So how does it belong to somebody who didn't go to war?

This is the exact place where many of you struggle. The tithe, the ten percent of your income, is not yours; it's God's. You are not *giving* to God when you tithe, you are *returning* back to Him what belongs to Him. If you don't give it back to Him, then you have robbed Him. That's why he said, "How will a man rob God?" (see Malachi 3:8). What is it that courses through your veins that would allow you to rob God of what belongs to Him? It wasn't yours, it's His. He said, "I'm not going to touch it, lest you say you made me rich."

What Abram was letting Melchizedek know was that, "If I held this, then what I'm saying to you is Satan is the one who's going to make me rich. Therefore, since I'm not willing to worship you, I'm going to give you what belongs to you. What I gave you now puts me in a position that you and God are my ultimate and I do not serve him because I'm not going to worship him. He might bless me now, but he will not bless me tomorrow. But God, as long as I keep Him first—because now I know where my blessing comes from."

Abram begins to tell Melchizedek, "Lest you say you made me rich." Do you realize that whatever he gave was enough to make somebody rich? He said, "I'm not going to hold this back from you lest you say you made me rich, and I'm not going to let you say you made me rich. I'm not going to let a job, let people, stuff, a house or a business tell me it made me rich. What I am going to tell you is the blessing of the Lord made me rich."

He literally goes on and says, "Take all except for what my young men have eaten and the share of the men, the allies who went with me, let them take their portion."

Genesis 14:15 says, "After these things..." You've heard TV announcers say, "We'll be right back after these messages." After the messages (which were really commercials), they'd come back. In those days it was only two or three commercials. Now it's like eight, nine, or ten— the commercials are longer than the program! But you knew that when the last commercial aired, they were coming right back. So when he said, "After these things," what was he talking about? What *just* happened. Abraham gave tithe to Melchizedek.

God said, "Okay. I told you to go and you went. I told you to keep peace, you kept it. You went into war; I told you to go and that I'd take care of you. You trusted Me to take the servants with you and you went and you won. Then, on top of that, in your level of obedience you tithed when it wasn't a law. Now I'm ready to talk to you about a couple things."

Abraham is not the faith father, he's the father of the faith. If you really study it through, you will find Abram did not do any one great feat of faith. I could go back through the scriptures and show you people who did very spectacular things by faith. It was not that Abram did one thing spectacular, however; it was that he lived a life of progressive faith. God told him to go; he went. As he went, he didn't know where he was going, but God was leading him somewhere.

He took Lot with him. God told Abram not to take him; he's not perfect. He lied about his wife; he's not perfect. He's making mistakes all the way through this thing, but God has been taking him one step at a time, one faith move at a time, one little thing this way: "Now I need you to do this; now I need you to do that." God's taking him through it. Finally, He says, "Now that I know that this money doesn't hold you, now that I know you'll give back to Me what belongs to Me, now I want to talk to you about some things."

After these things. God was saying, "I needed to see where you are." I've heard many people in their walk say, "I can praise, I can come to church, but I can't seem to get the tithe issue dealt with." You'll stay there. God's waiting after these things. "Well, I don't see it. I'm not getting it. It's not moving." You haven't gotten "after these things." You're in the second commercial, wondering, "How come they're not coming back with my show?" You're still in the second commercial!

He took him step-by-step.

Genesis 15:1 (AMPC)
"After these things, the word of the Lord came to Abram in a vision, saying, Fear not, Abram, I am your Shield, your abundant compensation, and your reward shall be exceedingly great."

Some of your translations may say, "I am your shield and your reward." The Hebrew words literally mean, *your quickly increasing salary.* The word of the Lord came to Abram and said, "I am your quickly increasing salary. This stuff isn't your salary, but I needed to know you weren't tied to it. If you're so tied to it, keep it, but you'll lose Me."

God didn't say Abram's servants were his salary. He didn't say as long as he kept going to war, he'd earn his money that way. He said, "I am your quickly increasing salary." Don't fear when you have just tithed and given enough to make somebody rich. He said "Fear not because everything you gave—I'm going to be your quickly increasing salary. Everything you just sowed, I'm going to be your quickly increasing salary."

Malachi 3:10 says that when you tithe, God will open the windows of heaven and He will pour out a blessing that you will not have enough room to contain it. Many people, when they hear that, think God is holding back their blessing and if they tithe, He'll let it out. That's not true. You are holding your own blessing. What is happening is, God keeps dropping it anyway.

Currency is the flow of money. The word comes from *current*. If you've ever swam in the ocean, you know a current can be strong. One time, my wife and I were at the Pacific Ocean in Oceanside, California. We started in one spot on the water next to the pier, and half an hour later we're like, "How in the world did we get so far from the pier?" It was the current, because current is fluid. When you don't have current, you put up a dam and the dam stops the current.

What God is saying here is, "Every day I'm still heaping blessings. The reason you won't have enough room to receive it is because it's shut right now. I'm still dropping stuff in the chute, you just ain't getting it." There comes a point where you do finally release that blessing, and it is so much that you don't have enough room to contain it. It's not that God doesn't want to give it to you, it's that you are damming up the pipeline between you and God with your little beaver self. You've built you a dam and you're like, "Isn't this pretty?" but God's like, "Really? Can we tear that thing down?"

I can tell you this much: you can never out-give God. I cannot tell you in a specific extrapolation or explanation as to how it happens. I can just tell you this much. When I learned to get my tithe straight, things opened up. I mean things like business, my life, my prosperity —things just opened up. I cannot tell you how. I can't sit down and say, "Well, x plus this, plus y, carry the one…" And I cannot tell you how I made less money but I have more. It doesn't make sense in the natural because it's the work of the Spirit. I can't tell you how I didn't get a pay raise at certain times, yet I was provided for and had all that I needed. I can't tell you exactly how it happened because it was the work of the Spirit.

> Genesis 15:2 (KJV)
> *"And Abram said, Lord GOD, what wilt Thou give me, seeing I am childless and heir of my house is this Eliezer of Damascus?"*

It's funny how the first question he asked was, "Okay God, I know You're courting me. You're talking about blessing me, but what can You give me? I need a child." God said, "I'm your quickly increasing salary and I'm your supply." He's courting him to cut covenant with Him and Abraham's response is, "I don't have a child." He was saying, "You've already blessed me so much that my tithe could make somebody rich. So I don't need any more. I have 318 servants! What I need is generational wealth. I need to be that righteous man who leaves an inheritance to his children's children." Personally, I believe it's a curse to die and leave your kids in debt, that every single generation has to start over.

Having been in real estate for many years, I've learned a lot about different people. Folks who had houses at the beach worth millions of dollars, many of them built by their grandparents or great-grandparents, received them because they were passed down. A righteous man leaves an inheritance to his children's children. It is a curse to have to start over with every generation. But still, Christians are so hemmed up about the idea of money and the idea of wealth that they're like, "Well, I don't want anything. We'll just get by." What do you do when the Bible says that a righteous man leaves an inheritance to not only his children, but his children's children? Should Jesus tarry and I step out of this world into heaven, it is my desire to leave an inheritance to my children's children. Sam Walton left money to his kids and wife and they're all still in the top ten of the world's richest people, even though it was split four ways.

Here's my challenge; Abram had enough money that his tithe could make somebody rich. Then God says, "I still want to do more for you because I see you are a man of faith." Not a man of doing great exploits, but he was faithful. So then Abram says, "Well, I don't have a child."

Now he's thinking, "If You're going to do more than what I've got now, I have to have somebody, because I have enough, more than I can spend in my lifetime. If You're going to do anything greater, if You're going to bless me beyond where I am today, then You have to give me some children. I will not be able to spend it in my lifetime, so they'll have to spend it in their lifetime."

What happens when you begin to think beyond you and into your generations to know that there are things God wants to do with your life and with your family that you won't be able to do? What if you were able to leave them with so much that they are now empowered to serve God with all that they have? I don't mean having enough money to paint your walls with liquid gold just because that's the stupidest thing you can think of. I'm talking about how God could use you if you weren't so worried about your light bill.

What could God use you to build? We could end world hunger. If God could just get enough Christians to get out of their poverty thinking, do you have any idea the churches we could build? We could compete against Disney as they're competing for the attention of your children. We could have universities and colleges where we could give education away. People could be well-trained and blessed in the Word of God, so they are not thinking that the world is without God! Do you have any idea, when the homosexual agenda is being pushed against the church, if we had some people with money longer than train smoke, we could shut that down!

Of course, we don't because we're too busy.

Jews are estimated to be 1 percent of the world's population, and represent 25 percent of the world's billionaires. In 2009, 139 (which is about 30 percent of the Fortune 500) were Jews. Thirty-five percent of the Nobel Prizes were awarded to Jews. I was thinking, "What in the world—?"

I remember Rev. Ricky (Dad) was speaking one day and he said that one of the ministers he knows was talking to a Jewish man. She asked him, "Why do all Jews think they're supposed to be rich?" He said, "I don't understand your question." She said, "I want to know why Jews think that they're supposed to be rich. What is it about them that makes them think they're supposed to be rich?" Again he replied, "I don't get your question."

I was sitting at lunch with Rabbi Allan Moorhead one day and I said, "Pastor Allan, tell me something." I told him the story, and I said, "I can't understand how this man didn't get her question. Does that make sense? Does that sound like a true story?"

He said, "Yeah, that makes a lot of sense. If they're an Orthodox Jewish family, every Friday night they do what is called the Sabbath Blessing. The first thing that happens is that the husband lays hands on his wife and pronounces Proverbs 31 over her. Then the wife lays hands on the husband and will cite Psalms 1:1. Then, they both will lay their hands on the children and pronounce the blessings of Abraham upon their life." He said every single Friday, they speak to their children growing up that they are blessed with faithful Abraham; that the Abrahamic blessing is on their life! They *know* they're supposed to be rich; they *know* they're supposed to be blessed! They're walking in it! It's not "What makes you think you're rich?" You are!

We were at Black Bear Diner and I could have ran home. I think I almost started to! All joking aside, I looked at him and said, "I have to go now. You shut this whole thing down." I paid for the bill and left.

Rabbi Allan said this to me as well. He said from a cultural standpoint, Jews have learned two things: 1) If they're extremely wealthy, they can be used to do what God needs them to do whenever He wants them to. 2) If they're the best at what they do, they'll never go back into bondage. You don't put the people who are the best in bondage. If everybody becomes a slave tomorrow, you best believe whomever the slave master is will find those who are good at stuff and bring them up out of the fields. If you are a good attorney, I don't want you picking turnips, I want you representing my house. They learn that if they don't want to go back into bondage, they better be the best at whatever it is they do and they rise above because they understand that the blessing of Abraham is on their life. It is the blessing of God that maketh rich and adds no sorrow to it!

MANIFESTATIONS OF THE BLESSING

Receiving the Promise By Faith

Galatians 3:13

"Christ hath redeemed us from the curse of the law being made a curse for us. For it is written cursed is everyone that hangeth on a tree."

This used to be the foundational scripture for the church that I came up in. I've read this I don't know how many times. I'm talking in the hundreds, possibly thousands of times, and it never clicked.

This is the beauty of the Bible. You can read something over and over again and have new revelation that comes just from continuing to read.

"Shutter Island" is a one-time movie. I can't imagine anybody seeing it twice. Once you've seen the end, that's a wrap. It becomes completely clear and nothing else about it makes it anything spectacular. When you get to it, you're like, "Really? That was it?"

My point is what separates the Bible from just a book is that it continually grows and lives in you. So even though you think you may have read the ending, you could read it again and get a whole new understanding. That's what makes the Bible alive. The value of it is not in its literary composition, but in its spiritual one. You can learn something new just about every time you read it. This is why you have to continue to develop in yourself the discipline of reading and studying your Bible. In this Book you will find greater degrees of revelation, even in the areas where you're like, "Well, I want to know which part I should read because whatever part I read, that's what I want to apply to my life." It doesn't matter which part you read. That's the spiritual nature of it. With a self-help book, you can go to the table of contents and see what you're dealing with. Then you go to that chapter, read it, and that's how you get help. With the Bible, because it's a spiritual thing, it doesn't matter which chapter you read. What matters is that you do it because through it God will speak things to you that He wants you to get and understand.

I've seen this I don't know how many times and I get the idea that I've been redeemed from the curse of the law. I am crystal clear that Christ has redeemed us. I understand my redemption. I understand I was brought back. I understand that I was purchased by the blood. I am crystal clear that I am redeemed from curses. The thing that I never saw was verse 14 which says, "So that…"

In other words, I have been redeemed *so that*. So what? For what reason was I redeemed? I was redeemed, not for the only reason of being set free from the curse, but I was redeemed so that the blessing of Abraham might come on the Gentiles. As the blessing of Abraham comes on the Gentiles, the only way it comes upon us is through Jesus Christ that we might receive the promise of the spirit through faith. So whatever this blessing is, we receive it through the spirit. It's not through natural things, it's not through your friends, it's not through your mama and others; it's through the spirit.

In the last chapter we looked at the idea that Abraham literally took his slaves and his servants in his house, went and fought a war with an army, then brought Lot back home. I wanted you to see the sign of the anointing: the anointing is the yoke-destroying, burden-removing power of God. Every one of you has an anointing. Every one of you has a yoke-destroying, burden-removing power of God resonate on the inside of you and on you. Once you're a born-again believer, the Holy Ghost is deposited on the inside of you. When we recognize that if you have an anointing, then the sign of the anointing is you are able to do more with less. In other words, if Samson was a huge, strapping guy with huge muscles, when he picked up the city gates and walked off with them, nobody would think anything of it. They would just say he's strong. Then when he picked up the city gates everybody was like, "Whoa!" Something about him did not match his situation. That was a sign of the anointing.

When you don't have all that you need, when you're not smart enough, when you're not gifted enough, that's when God needs to move so that He can demonstrate it was always Him and not you. So many people are waiting for God to do something and to move upon them to make them stronger; make them smarter and wealthier. What you don't understand is that when God moves, the sign of the anointing is to literally be that garbage guy living in a mansion.

Ephesians 3:20 says that God deals with us according to the effectual working of His power in us. He can do exceedingly, abundantly more than you could ask or think. The context of saying that He can do more than you can ask or think and that He works with you only according to what works in you means that God can move in your life only in accordance with what you can believe him for. So if you are a garbage man in a garbage man's body, you will get a garbage man's result (not that there's a problem with being a garbage man; if you're going to be one, be the best you can be). What He's telling us is that I could be a millionaire trapped in a different man's body. If I *can* be that, then whatever it is I can be is going to be relative to what I can *believe* Him for.

So many people say, "Oh, I'll never be able to afford a car like that." "I'll never live in a house like that, I'm only a—" "Well, you know, Pastor, you don't understand. I live on a fixed income." Who fixed it?

I get care packages every day. Stuff shows up almost every single day of my life. Who fixed it? What you can believe God for is what you currently have. Here, Abram goes out and destroys an army with some maids and butlers. That's a sign of being able to do more with less. The blessing of Abraham is not Abraham's blessing; it's the blessing that was on Abraham. It's obvious by Abraham's great exploits that he literally was able to do what no one else could seem to do. It was earmarked of the successes that he had that God was with him. When he and Lot got into it, God didn't tell him to take Lot but he took Lot anyway. Here, Lot's people are fighting with Abraham's people and Abraham said, "Look, we can't have all this strife. It's messing up my blessing."

Peace and unity was everything to Abraham—to the point where he said, "Look, we've got to talk. You take your people and go that way; I'll take my people and go this way. Or if you want to do the opposite, that's fine, too. Just tell me what you want to do and we'll do it because I can't have strife and contention. I can't have fussing and fighting and arguing going on in my house. If it goes on in my house, you are robbing me. I don't care which way you go." He added, "You can take the best with you, you can go to the best territories. I'll take the worst, because once I get the arguing, strife and contention out of my house, I could be in a barren land and the blessing on my life will overtake the barrenness and cause what is dead to produce. But I've got to get rid of the strife because strife will keep me from producing in either place. I can be in the best of lands, have a land flowing with milk and honey, but if we're fussing, fighting, arguing, and striving, you will steal my blessing."

If I'm in the world (I'm in the good land and everything is great, I'm living off of that), then when the land changes, so does my prosperity. When the recession came, people were buying houses right before that bubble busted (2003–2007) like they were going out of style. They were buying them with loans that gave people payments they couldn't afford. They were living high on the hog! (That's where the best cuts of meat are.) Then, all of a sudden the economy changed and these people lost their homes. What's bizarre is that they began to blame God for what society gave them, which is why society took it.

Abraham was saying, "I don't need the world to give me anything. You can take the best, Lot. You will need the best land because the blessing is not on you, it's on me. So you better go ahead and take the best because I can walk into nothing and the blessing that's on my life will turn it around into something." There's a company out there that's performing terribly and its price is just right because they're trying to give it away. You look at it and say, "I can't buy that company; they're not making any money!" The devil is a liar, because the blessing is on you! For some of you, the company you work for is still open because of you.

Abram went to war, took a whole gang of spoils, brought it back and he gave a tenth (his tithe) to Melchizedek. He made it clear when he said, "I've got to give this to you." The high priest Melchizedek said, "I don't want that, you keep it."

Abram said, "I'm not doing that, because I promised it to God. If I keep it, you'll be able to say you made me rich, so here's my tithe."

Hebrews 7:1-2 (KJV)
"For this Melchizedek, king of Salem, priest of the Most High God, who met Abraham returning from the slaughter of the kings, and blessed him, To whom also Abraham gave a tenth part of all; first being, by interpretation, King of righteousness, and after that also King of Salem, which is, King of peace;"

They're building something here. They're giving an explanation of Melchizedek, saying he's the king of Shalom, which is the King of peace, i.e. the Prince of peace.

Hebrews 7:3
"Without father, without mother, without descent, having neither beginning of days nor end of life, but made like unto the Son of God, abideth a priest continually."

What they're establishing here is that Melchizedek had no beginning and no end. He was the high priest continually, like unto our high priest, which is Jesus Christ, who is still a High Priest who has no beginning and no end. Notice they're drawing parallels here, trying to help you see by type and shadow what happened.

When Abraham brought his tithe, he brought it to Melchizedek, the one who brought him bread and wine. We understand this to be communion which is the responsibility of the priest. They're making this parallel to help you understand that in the same way Melchizedek was the high priest, you still have a high priest.

This is why when people get stuck on the idea of paying a tithe, the first thing I'll say is, "Take it to another church. If you have a problem with me talking about the tithe because you think I want something from you, take it to another church. Bring your *como se llama* here, but take your tithe somewhere else. When you see it start to work for you, then bring it to your hood where it does the most good." I know nobody will tell you to do stuff like that. No pastors are telling you to send your money somewhere else. You want to know why I can do that? Because I'm certain, absolutely certain, of what it can do for you and not to you.

Hebrews 7:4 (KJV)
"Now consider how great this man was, unto whom even the patriarch Abraham gave the tenth of the spoils."

The Amplified Version says, "Now observe and consider how great [a personage] this was to whom even Abraham the patriarch gave a tenth [the topmost or the pick of the heap] of the spoils." Most people say the tithe is under the law. The problem is, Abraham was the great-great-great-great grandfather of the Levites, which means there was no law in Abraham's time. Therefore, when Abraham tithed, he gave by faith. We are still people of faith who still have a high priest.

Hebrews 7:5
"And verily they that are of the sons of Levi, who receive the office of the priesthood, have a commandment to take tithes of the people according to the law, that is, of their brethren, though they come out of the loins of Abraham."

The children of Levi (the Levitical priesthood) were commanded to receive tithes by law. This tithe was brought to take care of the house of God and the people who were serving God. Then they were supposed to bring offerings to take care of alms and the poor. Your tithe can't go to help other people; that's not a tithe. Your tithe becomes a tithe only when it comes into the church to take care of the house and those who serve it.

Here's what's interesting: most pastors have to start other companies and do other jobs because the church expects them to live off of more faith than they're willing to. Therefore, the pastor's attentions are always divided because they have to run companies by day and preach the paint off the walls. Personally, I have been blessed, but I know many pastors who can't spend time preparing because they are working to feed themselves when their church should be feeding them.

Hebrews 7:6-9
"But he whose descent is not counted from them received tithes of Abraham, and blessed him that had the promises. And without all contradiction the less is blessed of the better. And here men that die receive tithes; but there he receiveth them, of whom it is witnessed that he liveth. And as I may so say, Levi also, who receiveth tithes, paid tithes in Abraham."

Hebrews is setting Jesus up as the High Priest; it's letting you know your obligation to Christ and to the body of Christ. While Levi was yet in the loins of Abraham, when Abraham tithed, Levi tithed, too. Even the charge given to Levites to receive tithe, they were the greater priesthood and that's why they had the charge. But it also says that the one who blessed Abraham was not even of the Levitical priesthood; he was of faith. The lesser was tithing to the greater!

It's interesting because the truth is, people think, "Well, it's under the law of the Levitical priesthood." No, he said the ones who received the tithe were lesser than the ones who gave it. God chose Abraham to bring the Levitical priesthood out and then told everybody, "Tithe to them because they're the greater who came out of Abraham, yet Abraham tithed unto the lesser." In Abraham, they tithed.

How can a generation tithe when they were not even born? This moves tithing out of a natural thing. I can't do it naturally because that would mean that I could take my future generations, birth them and their kids, and then tell them, "Here's your tithe; go give it to them," which I cannot do. That means it's a thing of the spirit.

Earlier I talked about the madman of Gadara running around cutting himself. Every time they chained him up, he broke the chains. He was possessed by demons which were able to give him supernatural strength. What we now know is that—from a spiritual standpoint—demonic things and demonic people can possess superhuman strength because they draw strength from the realm of the spirit. Yet, we still struggle with the idea that God can give you supernatural strength. Satan is a mere facsimile—a cheap one at that—who can do anything that God can do. Anything Satan can do, God can do better.

The question is, why do we clearly understand that demonic things can have supernatural power?

All power is spiritual in nature. If this is true, then why can't prosperity be spiritual in nature? You think it's a natural thing. "It's got to tie to my natural job. I have to work natural hours and I have to do natural things. I have to work extra hard and stay up until all hours of the night because if it's meant to be, it's up to me." Here's the thing: Levi says they were yet in the loins of his father when Melchizedek met him. That means Abraham, how he dealt with things, affected his future children, which now moves beyond relationship into covenant.

When he starts talking about generations, he has now moved beyond a conversation about "Me and the King of Salem was pretty cool." He's now talking about "We have covenant. Now my future generations shall be blessed because in me, when I was obedient and did the right thing, they did it with me." So now the blessing comes through the nature of having covenant, and this covenant cannot be broken. Have you ever wondered why there are two rings? The man gets a ring, the woman gets a ring, and if you put those two rings together, it forms an eight laying on its side.

An eight laying on its side is the symbol for infinity, with no beginning and no end. The two come together and form a covenant which says, "Till death do us part." Covenant is set and it's set for a reason. Here are the reasons for covenant: 1) Provision—to provide in an area of lack. When I cut covenant with my wife, she's supposed to bring something to the table and I bring something to the table. What she doesn't have, I'm supposed to have and what I don't have, she brings. Covenant is the idea that what you lack, I provide. This is why you can't have Adam and Steve. I don't care if you look at me in that tone of voice; it's biblical. I bring what you don't have, and when we come together, we become one. 2) Protection/safety—How many times do you see something on TV where something goes bump in the middle of the night and who jumps up? Not the wife! She's waking you up. "Honey, get up. Go see what that is and if you die I'll live to tell the story." If you, as a man, would send your wife, maybe that's why you're single. 3) Preservation—to continue a bloodline or a family name. So if we were to cut covenant together, I give you my last name, and that name continues on in my children (unless you have a progressive wife who says she won't take your last name with their Jezebel self). 4) Partnership—this makes sure the relationship is not taken advantage of.

Thus, the four Ps are: Provision, Protection, Preservation, and Partnership. From a marital standpoint, the husband isn't better than his wife; they're partners. They have different responsibilities. God will hold the man responsible, but that's to make sure the relationship isn't taken advantage of. He's not a dictator; he considers her opinions and what she wants, and he leads his house like Christ leads the church.

If I was a fighter/warrior, I could go to war and whoop some tail! But I couldn't grow vegetables for nothing. I can't grow them; I do not have a green thumb. I would find another tribe that couldn't fight their way out of a wet paper bag. I'd go to them and say, "Look, let's cut covenant together. Here's what we'll do. Anybody attacks you, they're attacking me. I'll protect you. But when my troops are hungry, it's your job to feed them." When we cut covenant, I'm saying, "What you dont have I have, and what I don't have I'm going to get from you. We're going to come together, put everything we have into the same pot, and we live off of that." Like the old presidential campaign slogan —a chicken in every pot. We're going to take care of each other.

Genesis 15:1 (KJV)
"After these things the word of the LORD came unto Abram in a vision, saying, Fear not, Abram: I am thy shield, and thy exceeding great reward."

At this point, God is courting Abram. He's like, "Okay, I watched you be faithful after these things." What things? Tithing to Melchizedek (which we just talked about). He continued, "When I told you to go, you went. You've been faithful in other areas, now you are faithful in your money. This was the last hurdle I needed to see and now I'm pretty sure you're the right guy. So now I want to cut covenant with you." Abraham recognized this and says, "What are You going to do for me seeing as I go childless?" God begins to go down this road of covenant.

Genesis 15:8-11 (KJV)
"And he said, Lord GOD, whereby shall I know that I shall inherit it? And he said unto him, Take me an heifer of three years old, and a she-goat of three years old, and a ram of three years old, and a turtledove, and a young pigeon. And he took unto him all these, and divided them in the midst, and laid each piece one against another: but the birds divided he not. And when the fowls came down upon the carcasses, Abram drove them away."

Abraham said, "How will I know that all You're promising is actually going to come to pass?" God began to instruct Abram in something that many of you have no conception of because it's not of our time. If you said, "Pastor, how do I know you and I are going to cut covenant?" and I said, "Go bring me these animals and let's cut them in half and lay them out," you'd be like, "…okay?"

What actually happened was, when they laid these animals out on the ground, the two parties who were cutting covenant would start in the middle of these animals with their backs to each other. One would stand facing one way, the other facing the other way. Then they would walk in a circle around the dead animals and end up facing each other (Two circles = infinity). They would say, "If I break this covenant, whatever we have done to these animals, let it be done to me," then they would cut covenant.

When God said, "Start cutting these animals up," He was telling Abraham, "I'm getting ready to cut covenant with you. So whatever you lack, I'm going to be your provider, your protector, your quickly increasing salary. I'm going to preserve My name through you and I'm going to set up partnership with you."

Genesis 15:14-18
"And also that nation, whom they shall serve, will I judge: and afterward shall they come out with great substance. And thou shalt go to thy fathers in peace; thou shalt be buried in a good old age. But in the fourth generation they shall come here again, for the iniquity of the Amorites is not yet full. And it came to pass, that, when the sun went down, and it was dark, behold a smoking furnace, and a burning lamp that passed between those pieces. In the same day the Lord made a covenant with Abram, saying, Unto thy seed have I given this land, from the river of Egypt unto the great river, the river Euphrates."

Here's the challenge I want to present to you: It says that a smoking furnace moved between the pieces. Here, God is courting Abram to set up covenant with him, and He is literally courting him. You know what courting is? You know, send them flowers, talk nice to them on the phone, trying to get his attention. (You know how people do it. Stop acting like you've never been there.) And in that, God is seeing something in him that He's like, "I like what's in him. I need to get him to a place where he understands I'm about to do some great things in him." The smoking furnace moved between the two pieces.

Genesis 15:12
"And when the sun was going down, a deep sleep fell upon Abram; and, lo, an horror of great darkness fell upon him."

This ceremony occurred while Abraham was asleep, yet God said "I'm going to cut covenant with you."

Hebrews 6:12-3 (KJV)
"That ye be not slothful, but followers of them who through faith and patience inherit the promises. For when God made promise to

Abraham, because he could swear by no greater, he sware by himself."

He made covenant with Abraham, but this says because He couldn't find anybody greater, He made covenant—or swore—by Himself.

Many people don't understand God the Father, Jesus the Son, and the Holy Ghost. They think Jesus stepped on the scene when He was born of Mary, but we know that not to be true. When Shadrach, Meshach, and Abednego were in the fiery furnace, Jesus showed up in the furnace. Therefore, He was not just born; he took on His earthly ministry through Mary, but He did not just show up through Mary. So when we see the smoking furnace moving through the pieces, it was not Abraham.

If I break a covenant with you, you have the right to do to me what we just did to these animals. The only way that God could get covenant which Abraham could never break is to cut that covenant with Himself. That's why He said He swore by Himself. In other words, that smoking furnace was Jesus cutting the covenant through the blood so you could never break what God put on him. If He made it with Abraham, Abraham's a flawed man. Therefore, if he messed up, he would deserve to die.

That means He said, "I couldn't find another person who could get this done so I swore by Myself. I won't break covenant with Myself."

Religious people are uncomfortable now. He said, "I will bless those that bless you and I will curse those that curse you. When I put my covenant on you, not only will I bless you to be a blessing, but I'll bless those who bless you." Now, whatever was on Abraham was so that the blessing of Abraham might come onto the Gentiles by the spirit by faith. Then the question is, *What in the world is it that came on you when you accepted Jesus as your Lord and Savior, and why do you still think that it has to do with you?* Even if you messed up, so what? Even if you didn't get it right, so what? It has nothing to do with you because you didn't cut the covenant. God said, "I couldn't do it by anybody greater so I did it by Myself."

So when He said that blessing the covenant, remember, the covenant has nothing to do with you. You're the benefactor. He said, "Look, Abram. I'm trying to cut covenant with you." But when He told him, "Look out to the stars and tell me how many you see. Look into the sand and tell me how many grains of sand there are," Abram couldn't tell him that, but God could. God was letting him know "so shall your seed be."

Now you know Abraham didn't have that many kids, so God had to be talking about something that was beyond Abraham. Once again, a work of the spirit. So shall your seed be. When Abram looked out and saw all the grains of sand, he saw you and me and those that come after and those that came before. God was telling him, "I'm going to bless the world through you because it's covenant."

If we have fruit of our relationship I am in covenant with the fruit of that relationship. Therefore, when my wife has children, my babies, I'll be in covenant with my babies. I'll be responsible to protect them and provide for them. If another man and his wife have babies, am I obligated to them? I'm not in covenant with them, but I'm in covenant with my wife. Therefore, we know that covenant spans generations. If he and I cut covenant where he's supposed to protect me and I'm supposed to cook for him, if anything happens to him, his family is still on the hook.

How many of you remember Mephibosheth? He ran—or I should say his wet nurse took him and ran—because she knew David was coming and she was afraid. So she hastily grabbed him and said, "We've got to get out of here. David's coming to occupy the castle and you ain't welcome because you're supposed to be the next in line. If

David catches you, he's going to hurt you." So she took Mephibosheth and ran, dropped him, and broke his leg. It never healed properly. Years later, David asked, "Is there anybody in the house of Jonathan that I can show kindness to?" What the nurse didn't understand was that David cut covenant with Jonathan, which meant Jonathan's child lived all his life away from the covenant. He could have been eating at the king's table, but because he ran from it he was injured by it. The very thing that could have been a blessing to him, he ended up living without until David sent for him. When he came, he said, "I'll just serve somewhere and I'll just do—"

But David said, "No, no. Nonsense! Get this boy, put the best robe on him. Give him everything that belongs to him, sit him at my table."

When you understand covenant, you recognize you have a right to walk in it or not walk in it. It's your choice! But when you come to God and you realize you are in covenant with Him, He says, "I don't need you to serve; sit at My table." And He prepares a table before you in the presence of your enemies because God said you have covenant with Him as a covenant child!

"Well, I'm not good enough. I messed up. I ran away." Bring your limping self to God because it doesn't matter what you've done. It doesn't matter how you've messed up because once you believe in Jesus, the blessing of Abram will come upon those who believe. And it's a work of the spirit, not of the natural.

"Well, I don't feel prosperous." Nobody asked you. "I don't look prosperous." You do to me. This book was written to the most prosperous bunch of people I've ever met in my entire life. "Well, I've done some stupid stuff." Welcome to the club, so have I. Trust me. You have no monopoly on stupid.

What was on Abraham now is on you. Whether you walk in it or not doesn't change whether it's there. So now we see Abram, Isaac, and Jacob. Isaac is in the middle of a famine. The Bible says he sowed in that land and reaped. How in the world could he be in the midst of recession; he's in the middle of famine. Everybody else is struggling. Everybody else is losing their jobs. Everybody else is in a recession. Everybody else is in an economic downturn. Everybody else but him.

It says that he sowed in the same land. He didn't go on a quest to find the best land and when he finds it, he plants there, digs there, sows there, and everything will be great. He sowed in the same place that the world was sowing. Yet he reaped and they didn't. How do you explain that my stuff is right next to your stuff, I give just like you give, I tithe just like you tithe, but yet when I'm faced with a situation that comes against my house and against my family and against my livelihood, I am absolutely convinced that there's a blessing on my life? Whatever that is that wants to take from me, it has no right to do so because I am a covenant child of God!

I give like you give. To be honest with you, I think I'm probably the sixth or seventh largest giver in the church so I'm not #1. I'm working on it, though. I'm competitive. I want to be #1 because nobody is going to out-give me except God. But here's my point: mine produces. I'm not better. There's no line in the Bible that says, "When pastors tithe and they give, their tithe is special. I have a special regard for theirs." It's not true.

"Well, God loves them more than me!" Stop. You know that isn't true. One knows they're blessed and the other doesn't. One expects the blessing on their life—cars, stuff, houses, businesses, and other things can all come. "Oh, that was such a blessing!" No it wasn't. It's a manifestation of the blessing that's on me and I'm going to allow this thing to manifest until it can't manifest anymore!

Paul said that God "can do exceedingly, abundantly more than I can ask or think according to the power that worketh in me" (Galatians 3:20). That means that whatever God is moving into my life is what I can believe Him for. Not what you can *ask* Him for, but what you can *believe* Him for. Some of you ask for stuff you don't believe you will receive. You know how you Band-Aid that? You say, "If it be Thy will."

"Oh God, bring a new home for my family if it be Your will." When it doesn't come, you can say it wasn't His will. This makes you feel better because it takes the pressure off of you. The reality is, it's what you are able to believe Him for. He said "he that comes to me must believe that I am" (Hebrews 11:6). I am what? Whatever you need. The Bible says the church should desire the best gift. What's the best gift? The one you need.

He ends it right there; "I am." He is what? Your healer, your victory, your provider. He said, "When you come to Me, you have to believe I am." Some people come and ask for healing but don't believe He's a healer. Some people ask for prosperity and don't believe He can prosper them. They think they have to get ten jobs. A woman came to me one time and said, "Pastor, we've got some things going on with our business and we need x amount of dollars. I need you to pray that we get that money." I said, "I'm not going to pray that you get that money because there's only one way that can happen. What I'm going to pray is that God shows up in the situation and resolves it." Within two weeks it was resolved, and it wasn't that God brought all the money necessary, He just changed what was needed.

When the blessing is on you, I don't need to tell God how to do it. Once I start telling God how to resolve my problems, I have yanked it out of the realm of the spirit and brought it down to the realm of the natural. But as long as I know that the blessing on my life shall produce, then how He gets it done is not up to me. "Well, Pastor, you know I'm facing this huge situation and I need ten thousand dollars." You only need that because the world told you you needed that. But my God, who makes everything, can turn the whole situation around just like that. However, we get so minded of ourselves, we lose the ability to see that it is the blessing of the Lord that makes rich and hard work adds nothing (see Proverbs 10:22). I was raised to work hard. I'm not advocating you don't work at all, because that's laziness. I advocate you work smart. But to sacrifice your own body to have something you'll never live long enough to spend, how can you tell me that's God?

"Work your fingers to the bone!" Really? Are you sure? Where's God in all that?

We violate laws all the time, not realizing God is not going to make you into a person who's going to have to suffer for the latter part of your years in order to make a living. He promised Abraham he would live long and die of a good, old age. Not a bad, old age but a good one. Still getting around, looking at all his kingdom, his children, all his grand-babies—a good old age.

Why do you find it so hard to believe that God wants you to live to a good old age, to be able to provide for your family, and literally prepare your children for the lives they're going to have? Why do you find that so hard to believe? You want to know what it is? Some of you have bad doctrine. Some of you have a spirit of poverty. "My family never had nothing, we ain't never had nothing. Grandmama never had nothing and my grandmama's grandmama never had nothing."

Seriously? How about we change that today. How about we recognize that the reason I was redeemed is *so that*. So when God says I'm blessed to be a blessing, I recognize that He's not going to prosper me just so I can have gold toilet paper. Some of you, if you got too much money too fast, you'd lose your mind. But what if you began to realize that He blessed you so that you could be a blessing? He prospers me so I can help others.

Some of you need to recognize this guilt trip people play on you. When you start doing well, things start changing, things start happening. You start going with God and things start getting better. You ever notice how there are one or two people in your family or your circle of friends who start talking about how you've changed? They have problems with it because you're prospering, right? Watch the little guilt trip they play. What they want you to do is to reach back and help them before you have fully gotten out. It's called crabs in a barrel. If you've ever seen crabs—I happen to love blue crabs and they're very hard to find here in Arizona since we're landlocked, but I love them when I get an opportunity to find them. When you put them in the sink, for the most part—I had one that broke this rule recently, but usually if you put them in the sink they can't get out. The moment they try to climb out, another grabs them and pulls them back in.

What will happen if you can't get out? Their goal really wasn't to get themselves out because they don't want to change; their goal was really to keep you from getting out. If you really want to help somebody, you have to get out first. Despite their feelings, despite their hurts, despite their ills, you've got to get out first. Then you can throw a lifeline if you want to. But what they try to do is get you to work with them before you fully get out.

Your future generations depend on you understanding this. Jews know this. This is not anything new; they know the blessing of Abraham is upon them. Their children know it from a young age. This is why they represent 1 percent of the world's population, yet 25 percent of the world's wealth. There has got to be something on them.

In a list of the top 10 youngest billionaires, 4 out of the 10 were made by Facebook, which was founded by Mark Zuckerberg.

I'm tired of other people being able to walk in what God has promised us. If the wealth of the wicked is laid up for the just, then where are the just? There are people like Warren Buffett who will never spend the amount of money he has, who has made the pledge that when he passes, most of his money is going into the Bill and Melinda Gates Foundation. Not into the church, not into anything remotely spiritual.

We need to wake up and realize that the wealth of the world is being jockeyed and positioned to remain out of our hands. My Bible tells me that the wealth of the wicked is stored up for the just. It isn't passed out to the just, it is stored up for the just, which means that we're gonna have to take it. How do we take it? By force? The force of faith. We have to learn how to walk in this. We have to learn how to get this poverty stuff off of our lives, to break ourselves free and break our families free, and realize that God expects and desires to bless us. If you have to work hard to get it, it most likely isn't Him. What He's waiting for is for you to chill.

"Look what I can do!" God can see what you can do. He's about to do something in your life that'll just bake your noodle. If you don't think my God is well able, I don't know what Bible you're reading. You might have the King Jimmy Crack Corn Edition. King Jimmy is like King James; you might have something close enough but it isn't the same. You might want to get one of the ones we read.

Can you imagine what God would do if you dared to believe Him? Could you imagine what He would do if you would just know that there's a blessing on you? That blessing will produce if you would just let it. I know you want to do something, I know you've been trained, "I've got to fix it!" But what would happen if you just step back and say, "God's got this. I ain't going to worry about it. God's got my next job. God's got my next house."

There's a house in this city with a double staircase coming down. That's my house. You see it, you let me know, because it's mine. Don't you move in it—unless you get two. Then you can have one and I'll take one.

You need to understand that there's a blessing on your life and it'll produce. Now, will it happen tomorrow? I don't know, but I'm in faith about it, and I'm going to stay in faith about it until that house shows up. I also have a Jaguar XJL on its way—white with a black panoramic top. It's on its way! Now, again, if you see it, don't you get in it and drive off in it—unless you get two.

I say this because I remember Dad Hagin shared this story one time. God was dealing with him about what kind of car to buy and he was struggling with some things. God said, "What kind of car do you think I want you to have?" Dad Hagin said, "I don't know." God said, "Whatever car you want." That's like one of those things that says, "If a tree falls in the woods, wherever it falls, there it is." As simple as it can be, He said, "What kind of car do you think I want you to have? Whatever you want."

What does it matter to Him? Do you think He wants you to have a car where you're struggling all the time trying to keep it going? Why would God want that to constantly drain your pocketbooks and your life so you can't do for Him what He needs you to do?

A year ago, I knew a woman who had no driver's license. Now, she has a license and a brand-new car. How does stuff like that happen? By faith. She walked into the dealership, did what God told her to do, but it didn't work so she left. The guy said, "No, don't leave," and she said, "I'm out of here." She went back, and they gave her exactly what God told her to get. Boom! Faith; it's in the realm of the spirit, a work of the spirit. It's not natural. This is not a natural thing. You don't need to be a stump about it.

Once you get your nice, new little car and somebody needs a ride but you don't want to give it to them because they have some little kids and they might have a lollipop or something and get it all over your nice Corinthian leather, you know you're wrong. Don't ask God for something that He can't use.

MANIFESTATIONS OF THE BLESSING

Heirs to the Blessing

Galatians 3:7-9 (KJV)

"Know ye, therefore, that they who are of faith, the same are the children of Abraham. And the scripture, foreseeing that God would justify the heathen through faith, preached before the gospel unto Abraham, saying, In thee shall all nations be blessed. So then they which be of faith are blessed with faithful Abraham."

It's important when you read a Scripture verse to also consider the context. Oftentimes when you begin to study Scripture on your own, you have to be very careful. You cannot take a verse and use it by itself without having context, without having an understanding of what the scriptures before and after are saying. Understanding the context brings a greater revelation and understanding so that you can stay on track. Many people have been taken off course because when they study, they pull one scripture out and make something of it. The reality is that you have to understand what the author is talking about and what the subject matter is.

Paul goes on in verses 13 and 14: "Christ hath redeemed us from the curse of the law, being made a curse for us; for it is written, Cursed is everyone that hangeth on a tree: That the blessing of Abraham might come on the Gentiles through Jesus Christ; that we might receive the promise of the Spirit through faith."

The context here is to help you understand who you are as a person of faith. So, if you believe in Jesus Christ, then you are of the faith. Paul makes it clear to go on to the next step that says you are a child of

Abraham. This means that the same blessing that was on Abraham now has the ability to be on you. So then when we read Galatians 3:13 that says "cursed is everything that hangeth on a tree," it goes on to help us understand that we've been redeemed from the curse of the law. Most of us, probably 90 percent of us, are clear that we've been redeemed. How do I know that? That's how you can get people to get up on stage, rap about, sing about, dance like, and dress like, but yet try to give glory to God. You act a certain way in your life and then you get up on a stage and say, "The first thing I want to do is thank God for blessing me."

You have to be redeemed to think that you could act, say, do, dress —you have to have a revelation of your redemption. I would venture to say to you—if I could say this very loosely—that they seem to have a better level of understanding concerning their redemption than most Christians. Now, the problem is that it goes off into the far side that says, "Well, God doesn't care how you act. God doesn't care if you come to church. God doesn't care if you believe. God doesn't care if you manifest what you believe. God just wants to know if you love Him." Somehow if you confess and say that you love Him, then that's good enough. The devil is a liar. But this is the prevailing thought and if you don't believe me, watch how people act. Watch how leaders— government officials, CEOs—watch how they act. They will just as quickly invoke the name of God and rob you blind in the process.

In my opinion, we have an overwhelming clarity of being redeemed from the curse of the law. Who wants to walk around saying, "Hey, I'm cursed"? Nobody. People say what? "Blessed." To some degree they have a level of cognitive understanding of what it means to be redeemed. Yet in its perfect application it becomes strewn in so many different directions. What the world wants you to believe is that it has become subjective to you so you can define what it is to be redeemed. That way, there is no way for people to judge you.

Paul says, "Christ hath redeemed us from the curse of the law, being made a curse for us; for it is written, Cursed is everything that hangeth on a tree." Why did Jesus become the curse for us? So that the blessing of Abraham might come upon us. The challenge is that what is cursed can't be blessed and what is blessed can't be cursed. So when the Bible says that Jesus came, He who was rich made Himself poor so that those who were poor could become rich. I know a lot of sanctimonious religious people want to say, "Well, he means rich in spirit." The problem is when you look up the actual Greek word that is used for rich and study it for yourself, you will find that word *rich* means "abundant in substance" not spiritually rich.

In the world, various things are blending together and now you can't tell what they are anymore because the lines are becoming blurred. Girls start dressing like boys, boys start dressing like girls, and we celebrate that because we've blurred the line. But God comes in and says, "I don't have any blurring. If you are cursed, you can't be blessed. If you are rich, you can't be poor. If you are poor, you can't be rich. If you're a girl, then you're a girl. If you're a boy, you can't be a girl." It is what He says it is and there is no blurring of the lines!

Here's the thing: we want to blur the lines because without contrast there is no knowledge of our errors. So we love blur; we do! "Oh, God's okay with it. He's all right. Besides, He knows my heart." Never mind the fact that out of the abundance of the heart the mouth speaks. You somehow think that what you do is not a manifestation of what's in your heart.

Here's why Christ redeemed us. He became the curse so we could become blessed. He said, "I became poor so that you could become rich." That must mean those who have become rich cannot be poor.

I cannot necessarily say that you're a fool if I don't know you, but I can tell if you're acting foolish. Just because you're acting foolish does not make you a fool. So many people act *impoverished*, but the only way I can bring you into *poverty* is to convince you that you're poor. He who is rich cannot be poor, yet I can act poor.

Christ said the reason He became cursed is so that the blessing that's on Abraham can come upon you through Jesus Christ and you become an heir to the promise. Verse 15 says, "Brethren, I speak after the manner of men: Though it be but a man's covenant, yet if it be confirmed, no man disannulleth, or addeth to it." In other words, if I bring you a covenant, it's just an idea until you and I confirm it. Once we confirm it, it now cannot be disannulled.

Galatians 3:16-18 (KJV)
"Now to Abraham and his seed were the promises made. He saith not, And to seeds, as of many; but as of one, And to thy seed, which is Christ. And this I say, that the covenant that was confirmed before by God in Christ, the law, which was four hundred and thirty years after, cannot disannul, that it should make the promise of no effect. For if the inheritance be of the law, it is no more of promise; but God gave it to Abraham by promise."

We understand the law as your behavior; what you do. You do the law. And we understand there's a curse of not doing what the law requires you to do. If you are not doing right by God, there are curses that come with your disobedience to Him. So what he's saying here is this particular promise is not, per se, covenant in the terms of it coming by the law. It was a promise in terms of faith because it came before the law. This means that if this covenant came before the law, then it is not taken out by it. Which then begins to imply that your performance and your behavior has nothing to do with the promise. He said because it's an inheritance, it didn't come by law, it came by promise. He said it was not to his *seeds*. Not everything you might want to believe is where your promise will come from. If you want to believe that all religions lead to God, you have missed it. He did not say *seeds*, He said *seed* which means there is only one way. You have to be careful because New Age spirituality is creeping into the church in such a way that it is causing harm. People are thinking about the light and enlightenment; worshiping the light and Buddha and all these other icons which are all dead and in the ground. But my God, Jesus Christ, is not dead. He is alive! That's why people will fight the name of Jesus! They'll say God, they'll say Lord, but when Jesus is mentioned they will censor that out because He is the only one by which the blessing comes!

He said, "To Abraham the gospel was preached." When God said "in you shall all nations call you blessed," He was preaching the gospel to him. That was way before Jesus in his natural form and way before Mary or Moses' existence. God was preaching the gospel to Abraham when He said, "Let me tell you something. Because you are faithful, in you shall all the nations of the world be blessed." Here's what He was telling him: If you convert over to Hinduism, you not going to be blessed, but if a Hindu converts over to Christianity, then the blessing shall come upon them! He said *all* nations! I don't care where you come from or what your background is, when you come into the family of God, you are blessed with faithful Abraham! That gives you the right to access all that God has for you! All the nations in us are blessed, but we are not blessed in all the nations.

God said they'll get it by faith. That helps us understand that prosperity is not so much what you do in the natural. Prosperity comes by what you do in the spirit. People will come to me and invariably most everyone at some point in time will ask me this question: "Pastor, I'm struggling. What should I do?" My answer is always the same; it's never changed. I say, "Keep coming to church." In their heads it's like, *I asked this guy for something that would help me and he gave me an answer that makes no sense.* To them, prosperity is a thing of the natural. For me, it's a work of the spirit. So what they wanted from me was a natural answer. They wanted me to tell them to get another job with what time they have available, to make their family suffer so they don't get to see them anymore. Then once they get enough saved, they can quit all those jobs and everything will be all right. That's what

49

people, to some degree, want me to say. But that's a natural answer where a solution never comes. It keeps you working towards an outcome that Satan can mix up and keep you stuck.

If you are saved and have been trying to get out of debt for years, but haven't been able to do it, why has it eluded you? I got out of debt in two years when I was making $400 a month. It's not a work of the natural. Let's put it this way: it can be, for you, a work of the natural, but you'll have to work the natural. For me it's a work of the spirit. He said that by the spirit is how it's obtained. "That he might receive the promise of the spirit through faith" (v. 14). That means this is not hard work, although we should work.

This is why people fail. They are trying to do in the natural what God expects you to do by the spirit. If you want to be more prosperous in what you are doing, learn spiritual activities. Learn how to give and sow. Learn how to serve. Learn how to attend. These are things that you may think have nothing to do with your prosperity, but they have everything to do with it.

When I make a decision to serve God and not money, when I have to face that moment where my boss says, "We need you to come into work today," and I'm saying, "I ain't coming in to work today," and he says, "Well, we're going to have to fire you," then I'll have to do what I have to do. The God I serve will honor every commitment I make for Him. He said, "Whatever you give up for Me, I'll give it back to you a hundredfold because sacrifice has to be made." But some of you are so afraid. You're afraid because you don't know that it is the blessing of God on your life that makes you rich and adds no sorrow to it!

It's a promise. He said, "If I make it a covenant, then you have to respond. But if I make you a promise, I'm responsible to keep it."

Let's say I make you a deal and I say to you, "If you come and give me five dollars, I'll give you twenty dollars." Then we write it up in a contract. In that contract I say, "If you give me five dollars, I now owe you twenty dollars," that's a contract. Now, do I owe you $20? Only if you give me $5. If you don't give me $5, do I owe you a thing? No. Once you give me the $5, do I now owe you by contract? Yes. But if I promise you that I'm going to give you $20, do you owe me $5? Does it have anything to do with you? No. I made a promise; do I owe you? Yes. If you act like a fool, do I still owe you? Yes. If you crawl underground, stay there for 30 years and come back, do I still owe you? Yes.

That means when I make you a promise, it has absolutely nothing to do with you, your behavior, or performance. If you are in faith and you believe in Jesus Christ, then you now are a child of Abraham so that the blessing of Abraham might come upon you. It has nothing to do with your abilities, your cuteness, your fondness, your aptitude, your intelligence, your abilities, your skill sets; it has nothing to do with any of that. I made you a promise.

Some of you are like, "Promises don't matter to me." That's because you've been burned by people. You've allowed your trust to become affected by people you have dealt with in the past. If you're not careful, you'll begin to think your natural father is like God. You'll begin to think your baby daddy is like God. You'll take substitutive people and place their character in light of God. What you should be doing is recognizing that God is God all by Himself. He says He'll never leave you or forsake you. He's not a man who will lie. If He can't lie, then even if what He said doesn't look like what you have, if He is one who can call those things that are not as though they are, the moment He said it (because it wasn't so) would imply that He lied. But the Bible says that He's a man who cannot lie.

Most people live in this place. "I know God said that, but that's not in my life. Pastor, what are you talking about? I can't see that." I know, you can't see it because you think God's a liar. It's sad, but you do. It happens in the moment you realize it is quite possible that what you have doesn't line up with what He said. Let's just say you weren't there when He said it. The moment you heard it, if it is against what you have, He now substitutes your truth with His and it becomes so. This is why the Bible says that people have to hear it.

"I know what the Bible says, Pastor, but that ain't real." You're calling my Daddy a liar. When He said that the reason Jesus went to the cross, He said it was *so that* the blessing of Abraham shall come upon the Gentiles. The reason the cross happened was so that the blessing could happen. The reason why we do this is so that this can happen. The reason why we give is so that this can happen. The reason why we serve is so that this can happen. The reason why we attend is so that this can happen.

Have you ever heard the expression, "They were born with a silver spoon in their mouth"? For almost every one of you, that invokes some level of disdain. "They don't know what it means to work. They were born with a silver spoon in their mouth." You look down on them because you're like, "That's just terrible." I was watching a show about children and parents. One of the children was continually called a nerd. The parents decided that they wanted to have their kids around more influential and social elite people, so they took their son to a party of socially elite people (aristocracy). The little boy was talking to another little boy at the party about his age, and the second boy asked, "Aren't you afraid people are going to call you a nerd?" The first boy said, "Nerd? Let me tell you something. We are the future captains of industry. We're going to be the next senators and the next CEOs and presidents in this world. I have no worry about being called a nerd." Because he was so intelligent, gifted, and talented, he deemed being called a nerd negative because of the circles in which he travelled.

But then he got into a different circle where they had the same experience but a whole different view. They're like, "Nerd? What do you mean nerd? Bill Gates was a nerd. Warren Buffett was a nerd. Are you kidding? These are captains of industry. These are people who can write checks and the bank bounces!" Two different worlds, same experience.

What ended up happening is that daughter of the family got hooked up with some of the daughters of these wealthy people. They ended up convincing her to shoplift, which obviously with their wealth they didn't need to do. But they did it anyway because they needed danger, trouble, and something to get into. As the story unfolded, you began to realize even though these people were wealthy, they still struggled with the same character flaws. So it wasn't really that they were better; they just had a different understanding.

We all rally around the idea of, "I can't believe it. They were born with a silver spoon in their mouth. They don't know trouble, they haven't seen any problems. They don't know what it's like. Child, I've had to struggle all my life and they never had to do any of that. I don't even like her! I don't like him. They don't know what it's like. Man, if they lived in my life for one moment, they would just give up. They'd just throw in the towel."

We're agitated by the idea that someone has had a leg up. But then if I asked you this question, "How many of you parents want your children to be better off than you?" and you answer you do, you're a hypocrite. The ones born with the silver spoon in their mouth, their parents paid the price so that their children could have a better life. You talk about your children having a leg up and having a better life, but when others have it, you look down your nose and say they were born with a silver spoon in their mouth.

This is the hypocrisy that lives within us. We don't even see that it is a curse to have to start over with every generation. You're in this holy piousness of "God didn't say that we all should be rich and we should just settle for what we don't have."

Genesis 25:29-34

*"And Jacob sod pottage: and Esau came from the field, and he was
faint. And Esau said to Jacob, Feed me, I pray thee, with that same
red pottage; for I am faint: therefore was his name called Edom.
And Jacob said, Sell me this day thy birthright. And Esau said,
Behold, I am at the point to die: and what profit shall this
birthright do to me? And Jacob said, Swear to me this day; and he
swore unto him: and he sold his birthright unto Jacob. Then Jacob
gave Esau bread and pottage of lentils; and he did eat and drink,
and rose up, and went his way: thus Esau despised his birthright."*

The father's blessing is the blessing that comes from the father to
the firstborn child in order to impart the Abrahamic blessing. Abraham
undoubtedly blessed Isaac and then Isaac was supposed to bless Esau.
It says Abraham, Isaac, and Jacob. Did you ever hear somebody say,
"I'm pulling your leg"? When Jacob was born, he was holding onto
Esau almost as if he was trying to pull Esau back in, because they were
twins. So whichever one was born first would have been the firstborn.
That's where you get the phrase "pulling your leg" because Jacob
means "trickster." Interestingly enough, Esau is out in the field where
he's been working all day. He comes in and he's famished. He says to
Jacob, "I'm hungry; give me some of that stew you got there."

Jacob says, "If you sell me your birthright, your blessing, I'll give
it to you." Esau said, "Okay." Then Jacob said "Swear right now!"
Have you ever dealt with someone you didn't want to think too long
about stuff they agreed to do? "You should lend me some money." "Oh
yeah, I'll do that." "Okay, can I have it right now?" You know if they
get out of your sight, you might not see it again.

Here these two brothers are having this exchange about the
birthright and Esau says, "I'll give it to you." He swears by it and he
gives it over to Jacob. The Bible says he despised it. His answer was,
"What good is this blessing if I'm going to die?" He had a natural

problem, and he had a spiritual solution but he was unable to connect the two.

Hebrews 12:16 MSG
"Watch out for the Esau syndrome: trading away God's lifelong gift in order to satisfy a short-term appetite."

I've seen many people end up in a relationship trying to satisfy a short-term appetite and, in doing so, they gave up the long-term plan of God for their life. What he was saying was, "Be careful. Is there any fornicator or profane person as Esau?" To fornicate means to have relations with multiple people who are not your wife or your husband, or to have sex with someone, male or female, that is not your husband or wife. So therefore, he's saying you are having intimacy with something or someone that is not in covenant with you. You are more intimate with what is not in covenant with you than you are with the one who is. This makes you a fornicator and a profane person as was Esau who for one morsel of meat sold his birthright. He gave up his blessing. Esau later regretted that impulsive act and wanted God's blessing, but by then it was too late. Tears or no tears. He traded God's blessing. He traded God's direction. He traded God's favor for his appetite, for this fleshly thing he had to have. He said, "Now it's too late."

Romans 9:9-13 (KJV)
"For this is the word of promise, At this time will I come, and Sarah shall have a son. And not only this; but when Rebecca also had conceived by one, even by our father, Isaac; (For the children being not yet born, neither having done any good or evil, that the purpose of God according to election might stand, not of works, but of him that calleth), It was said unto her, The elder shall serve the younger. As it is written, Jacob have I loved, but Esau have I hated."

Before Rebecca gave birth, God said the older shall serve the younger. She knew it from jump.

I've always heard the story told in a way that blames Jacob for what he did to Esau. So here's my problem: if Jacob is the one who did something wrong and he bamboozled his brother, why would you love him and hate the one that got taken? That's almost like me saying I love the person who mugged you more than I love you. That makes no sense unless I'm the mugger's mother. You know how that goes. "My baby didn't do that!" Yes, he did. "No, he didn't! He's a good kid!" Right! He's been robbing people since he was 2 years old.

God said that Esau despised his blessing. Esau had the blessing, but he didn't care anything about it. He didn't even understand its value because he said, "What good is it going to do me if I die?" Never coming to the realization that the blessing would keep him from dying. So he had the blessing, it was his right to receive the blessing, he was the one who was blessed, and he was the appropriate and proper person to walk in the blessing. Yet because he didn't understand it and didn't use it, God said, "You have despised it. So now let Me give it to somebody who wants it." They were twins, born at the same time! They had the same DNA. There was nothing different between them other than one wanted the blessing and the other didn't. One sought after it, the other didn't. Whether Jacob did right or wrong wasn't the question. He wanted it so bad and his brother despised it so much that he said, "I'll do whatever it takes to get this blessing to come on my life. Once I'm walking in it, nothing can stop me. I'll sell this whole pot for one blessing."

"I'm hungry, so just give me a bowl and I'll eat for a moment." One lust, one appetite, and Esau walked away from the blessing.

You see people who say, "Pastor's got a nice house. That sure is a blessing." No, it's not. There is no *thing* that's a blessing. You could say, "That soup sure was a blessing!" If the soup was a blessing, then what was Esau crying about? That soup evidently was not the blessing. If we're not careful, we'll look at stuff and begin to believe that the stuff is the blessing. Everything that comes into my life is a manifestation of the blessing. So that means if I am blessed, then the blessing on my life (as a work of the spirit) will begin to produce things that are in line with my desires. They'll produce things for my children. A righteous man will leave an inheritance to his children's children. When the Bible says that, are you in a position to leave an inheritance to not only your children, but your children's children, or does your family need to have a yard sale to put you in the ground?

That's why Abraham said, when God wanted to cut covenant with him, "How are You blessing me, seeing I have no child? I'm already blessed by you. You've already empowered me to prosper. You've already made me wealthy. You made me so wealthy that my tithe, ten percent, could make somebody else rich. I already have more than I can spend in a lifetime. So if you're going to do anything more for me, you're going to have to give me some children."

I know this is messing up your theology on poverty. I'm doing that intentionally because I want you to put down what you think and pick up what God said. Now, all I have to do is stay focused on doing what God has asked me to do. I don't need more money, I need more anointing. I don't need more stuff, I need more God. I don't need more things, I need more Him. When I seek after Him, then I get clarity about the idea that He is a rewarder of those who diligently seek Him. He is a rewarder to them because they're going after Him. They're not looking for stuff, they're seeking His righteousness first and all these other things will be added by the blessing that is on their life. They don't have to go after it. He'll give it, but they have to come after Him. He has to become first in their life. He has to become the premier in their life. He has to be the one who directs their life. He said as long as He's first in their life, that He'll add the rest. Proverbs 10:22 says "The blessing of the LORD it maketh rich," And the writer added, "no sorrow with it." One translation says, "And hard work adds nothing to it."

Are you supposed to work? Yes. Are you supposed to get off into toil? No. What is toil? When is the last time you've seen your family? When is the last time you've been able to spend all this money you're trying to make? When's the last time you've been on vacation? The Bible says on the seventh day God rested. I have a sabbath; my sabbath is Monday because I work on Sundays. My sabbath is a 24-hour period of time in which I'm not going to be bothered by you. I'm not saying that to be mean; it's the truth. Do you have a sabbath; a 24-hour period of time in which you do not engage in work? You say, "Pastor, I can't afford to do that." You can't afford *not* to. That's how you know you're in toil. When your life is so hectic that you can't find 24 hours to spend with your family doing godly things, that's how you know you're in toil. If you keep trying to figure out a way to get to church because there's so much going on, you're in toil. If you can't even take a day and give it to God, that's how you know you're in toil. If you're in toil, the blessing of the Lord maketh rich and adds no sorrow to it. If toil adds nothing to your prosperity, then why do you do it?

Romans 9:11
"(For the children being not yet born, neither having done any good or evil, that the purpose of God according to election might stand, not of works, but of him that calleth.)"

Paul said for the children being not yet born, God said one will serve the other. They hadn't been born yet, haven't done anything wrong, haven't done anything good; they are just in the womb. They haven't even touched ground yet and God has already said, by election, this is what's going to happen: the younger will be the boss over the older. It says it wasn't according to works. All that transpired wasn't a byproduct of works or what they did. For Esau to despise his birthright and for Jacob to be hot after it and want it so bad, God said all that transpired with them was not why He said what He said. He said it was because He said what He said that all this transpired. Now, when you think of Pharaoh (the Bible says God hardened his heart), the Bible says He set him up. That doesn't mean He birthed Pharaoh to die, but it means that God knew Pharaoh was going to set himself against Him.

In John 9, when Jesus heals a man born blind, the people asked Jesus, "Hey, this man is blind. He's been born blind. Who sinned, him or his mother?" Jesus didn't say, "Why would ya'll bring up sin?" He said, "Neither." Notice, the disciples had equated the man being born blind with sin. They thought for this man to struggle with this sickness, he must have done something wrong. Since he was born that way, who did it? He couldn't have done it in his mother's womb. So was it his parents who sinned and, therefore, because they sinned so bad against God, now he's born with this? Jesus said, "Neither." The reason why he was born blind, the reason he went through what he did was *so that* the works of God may be made manifest in him. In other words, so that the blessing should come upon him.

Without poverty, it's hard to understand wealth. If you've been poor and become rich, you have a whole different understanding of wealth. I've been poor and I've been rich. Rich is better.

I know you think I've written something sacrilegious, but it's not. Rich is better. You still have problems, but when you have money, you have options. You don't believe me? Have you ever seen some of these wealthy people who contract sickness and disease and don't look any different? How do they do that? Money. If I wanted to debilitate the church and I was Satan, the way I would do it is to keep you thinking it's ungodly to be poor. What I'm now doing is taking away your options.

He said for the children not being yet born (Jacob and Esau), neither having done good or evil, that the purpose of God according to election would stand. Whatever God purposed, He called it already so that it would stand. Now, Jacob became Israel and Esau is the father of the Edomites. Here's the challenge. He said, "In Jacob I loved, but Esau I hated." How come? Esau did good things. The Edomites even prospered and Israel prospered, but Israel was so disobedient!

It was not their works or what they had done, but of Him who calleth. They both did right and they both did wrong, but because God calleth him, His blessing stayed. It was not because of him, it was because God is the one who stood on high and calleth it out before they were even born that they would be blessed. It has nothing to do with their natural abilities, but because God elected them. He also put that blessing on your life.

You didn't earn it, you don't even deserve it, but because God called it, that's why you deserve to be blessed. That's why you get to walk in the blessing, because He called it. And whatever He called shall stand. Nothing to do with works. Nothing to do with the stuff. You have a choice. You can stay rooted in your gospel of poverty and I'll love you just the same; just quit asking to borrow money from me.

I can give you a pot of stew or I can teach you how to manifest the blessing. I don't know about you, but I'd much rather you show me. I don't need you to give me a fish; I need you to teach me how to fish. What if you're not around? I need to be dependent on what God has given me. I'm not moved by natural circumstances and outward people. For me, I know it's the blessing that's on my life that produces whether you want to bless me or not, whether you like to be involved or not, whether you like me or not. It doesn't matter because it's the blessing of the Lord that maketh rich and adds no sorrow to it. It's the blessing on my life that will produce for me. It's the blessing on my life that will resolve problems and literally manifest what it is I need. It's the blessing on my life; it has nothing to do with people, their opinions, the stuff; it has everything to do with what God said. The blessing of Abraham might come upon me when I believe in Christ. All I have to do is take Jesus in my heart. Once I do that, I am now blessed like Abraham was blessed. Now I can strut like Abraham could strut. Now I can walk like Abraham could walk. Now I can win a war with some maids and servants like Abraham won a war. I can live unto the blessing of God in my life and nobody gave it to me. Therefore, nobody can take it from me.

It has nothing to do with you. Sometimes the decisions you had to make were purely because God wanted to know if you'd choose them or Him. Do you choose Him, or her? Do you choose Him, or him? Do you choose Him or that? "Well, you don't understand; I have bills." Nobody told you to live in an apartment and drive a Bentley. Get rid of that Bentley and get a nice car. Some of the problems you have, *you* put yourself in. When you allow Him to bring things into your life, He'll bring it, but are you patient to wait, or do you want it in your time because you have an immediate appetite?

I'm the first to tell you that when I get hungry, I get irritable. If I'm really hungry, watch out! My wife protects me from that stuff because if I get hungry, everything gets on my nerves. But I'll tell you what I won't do: I won't trade my blessing for it. I don't have Esau syndrome. I'd be like, "You want what? You keep your meat. My Daddy shall supply all of my need according to His riches in Christ Jesus. I tell you what: the Bible says those who bless me, God will bless them. If you'll just give me that pot of stew, you'll get blessed. But if you don't, that's fine. You can leave me out here by myself. God will find a one-legged mule to find my dinner. Whatever I command out of that blessing, it shall come to pass. I will not be left here without having anything. My God will supply all of my need and He'll do it when I need it. I believe in Him, I trust Him, not you. So give me some of that stew before I get angry. But I ain't going to give you what belongs to me because the fact that you want to sell it to me tells me you are not trying to bless me."

Some of you would do well to know where your blessings come from. You're trapped in situations where you only respect people who abuse you. You have become so dysfunctional, you can only appreciate an abuser. "He's just too good of a guy. He's a nice guy." What's wrong with a nice guy? You want your kids to marry a nice guy. You want your sons to marry a nice girl, but you can't find one. Hypocrisy. It's because dysfunctional thinking has allowed you to think that the good guys are the bad guys. Somehow in your head you have twisted it to think you like the bad boy and you can't deal with the good one. But then when the bad boy is sitting at home playing video games, you say to your girlfriends at work, "I wish he'd get a job, girl!" Why? He has a job—you. You let other people live off of your blessing that you don't even know you have. But they know the blessing that's on your life and that's why they were drawn to you.

The only thing I have to do is God. He said *all* other things. Do you know what "all" means in Hebrew? It means "all." He said *all* these things. What things? The things you have need of. We make this so complicated. What bothers a lot of you is that what really brings light and understanding for you is that I make it simple because it is simple. You have to be careful because if you start not recognizing people that you have no favor with, you'll get caught up with folks trying to gain their favor. This is why, ladies, you can get pulled into a sexual relationship before a man evidences commitment. You want commitment and you're trying to gain favor. So you do what it takes to try to gain favor because your assumption is if he won't commit, then you don't have favor with him. And you're right! But the problem is you don't get it by sleeping with him. That's why, even though you've been in a relationship with that guy, he leaves you and marries somebody else.

You need to cut out people who are not in favor with you. You will know immediately as soon as you need them that God has given you favor with those people in your life. The ones you don't have favor with, you need to cut them out of your life. Let them go, send them on their way. Send them packing; they're no good! Begin to recognize the ones you do have favor with, where they're in your life because they're blessed. My wife is blessed; she's beautiful, she can sing, she has a degree, and she's intelligent. I'm blessed; I have a degree, I'm intelligent, I'm good-looking. I'm blessed, and she's blessed. She's not in my life to hijack my blessing and I'm not in hers to hijack her blessing. I don't need her, I want her.

Why is that so important? There are people in your life who you think you need, but the moment you come to that conclusion you need to be careful. You are now saying that the blessing on your life is not enough. I don't want to be with someone who needs me. If my blessing's the only one that's working, it's enough. But how much more can we accomplish if I can get her blessing to start working? She's got that covered. I have mine covered. When we come together, that's double for your trouble. You now have two people who are firing all six cylinders. That's where the blessing really starts to produce and now you can see why God said, "Don't be yoked with an unbeliever." I don't care what they say; if they're not a genuine believer, that blessing is not working on their life. Now you're gimping along at half speed. But wait until you get all your tires on your car, get that puppy into fifth gear, and start moving down the highway of life with a partner who can produce.

Some of you have leeches who are just trying to get a little bit from your blessing. I wanted it, so I put a ring on it. It's that simple. If you won't put a ring on it, you don't want it. You want to borrow it, you want to rent it on the weekend, you want to drive it around town with the top down. The blessing is real and if you believe in Jesus, it's on your life. You have a choice of whether you walk in it or not. You have a choice whether you tap into it or not.

When I went to buy my car, before I walked in there I said, "Thank God I've been delivered from unreasonable and wicked men." Then along comes somebody wicked. I'm like, "Thank God I've been delivered from wicked and unreasonable men." Then right after he came over and introduced himself, his manager came out (who was a

Christian). He's become a very good friend of mine; he's a strong believer. He's the one who made the deal for me and gave me exactly what I wanted.

I always confess that I have been delivered from wicked and unreasonable people. Why? Because I have! Everywhere I go, my blessing has gone before me. I don't expect to do like you do. I'm not going to fight, argue, and hassle. I'll give you an example. Little Skippy, the first salesman I met, called me and said, "You going to bring that car back?" They told me to take it. They hadn't done the deal yet and told me to take it. The puppy dog close: take it, you'll love it and you'll keep it. Not this guy. Puppy dog close doesn't mean nothing to me because all puppies do is eat, sleep, and well, you know. I don't have a puppy for that reason. Now, if you get me a puppy with a job I can lease him out during the day as a seeing-eye dog. That's my puppy.

The salesman I've been delivered from calls me and says, "Are you going to bring that car back?" I said, "Sure, I'll bring it back today." The manager calls me back and says, "Keep it, we're still working on it." The salesman calls me again the next day. "You going to bring that car back today?" I said, "Talk to your boss! Stop calling me." So he goes and talks to his boss and I never heard from him again. The next call I get was a couple days later that said, "We got you a deal. Come on down and sign." I was driving the car for a whole week. Do you understand you're blessed?

If you get nothing else from this, please understand you are blessed. What the world wouldn't do for somebody else, they'll do it for you. You're blessed and that means you now have to pay attention to people who want to get in your life. Some people are just there to steal the blessing that you don't even know you have. They're on assignment, and I don't care if you think you don't feel blessed. It has nothing to do with how you feel. It's according to the election and purpose of God, which He purposed since the foundations of the world. You can walk in it or not. But if you don't, then quit asking God to bless you.

Someone that used to attend SCC a long time ago posted this on social media: "I'm standing in need of a blessing." What are they talking about? I know they know better! We don't stand in the need of a blessing; we are blessed! Why are you blessed? So you can go around sprinkling gold dust in the air? No! God told Abraham, "You are blessed to be a blessing."

MANIFESTATIONS OF THE BLESSING

Lord of the Sabbath

Galatians 3:13

"Christ hath redeemed us from the curse of the law, being made a curse for us: for it is written, Cursed is everyone that hangeth on a tree:"

Galatians 3:13 is certainly a foundational scripture that brings us to a place to understand all that Christ has done for us. We know that when we deal with Matthew, Mark, Luke, and John—the Synoptic Gospels—- that's the story of what has happened all the way through, how Jesus did what He did when He came historically. Then the Gospels bring us to the Epistles—the Epistles are the letters that were written. They bring us clarity as to *why* Jesus did what He did. It's important for you to know and understand historically what happened. But if I told you what happened and never told you why, there's no value to it. The application comes not in you having information, but having transformation. The difference between information and transformation is application. I can give you some great statistics, facts, and stories but if you can't apply them, then what's the point? You never experienced transformation.

In the book of Galatians, Paul writes that "Christ has redeemed us from the curse of the law, being made a curse for us: for it is written, Cursed is everyone that hangeth on a tree" (Galatians 3:13). We understand "hanging on a tree" means *hanging on the cross*. If you go to the book of Deuteronomy, you will see that there are many curses that come with violation of God's law. Many of them are related to areas of relationships, healing, prosperity; however, they are curses that will hinder you in your life by your disobedience to God. The Bible then tells us that the reason Jesus came is to redeem us from that curse. To be redeemed means that if go buy a product and I give them a coupon for a dollar off, guess what they give me? They give me the dollar. I have now redeemed it. That piece of paper alone is not worth a dollar. In most copy centers I can get a sheet for three cents. So the paper I gave them is not worth the dollar, the worth is in its redemption.

You're not worth a nickel; neither am I. But your redemption is. Jesus died so that you may live. When He redeemed you from the curse of the law, that means that what comes with the curse is no longer valid in your life or applicable. Whatever punishment you actually deserve, you now do not have to suffer the penalty because He took it. In the moment that He laid His life down for you thousands of years ago takes away everything you did, will do, have done, about to do, thinking about doing, praying not to do, hoping not to do. You know what you should do but you do the thing you weren't supposed to do when you wanted to do it, but after you did it, then you did it again and swore you'd never do it.

All of that was laid on Him so "that the blessings of Abraham might come on the Gentiles through Jesus Christ, that we might receive the promise of the Spirit through faith" (Galatians 3:14).

We are so clear about our redemption. We've been redeemed from the curse and penalty of the law. We can rally all around that. But do you ever realize that there was a reason why all of that sin had to come off of you? It's so the blessing could come on you. You can't go into Egypt, learn what Egypt teaches you, become an Egyptian, and then go into your promised land acting like an Egyptian.

You've probably heard the saying, "You can take the brother out of the hood but you can't take the hood out of the brother." There's some truth to that. If you walk into your blessing acting like you're cursed, you will negate the blessing by virtue of the curse. The Bible says out of the same mouth blessing and cursing can spring (see James 3:10). Then He says but that's not so concerning water. He said a water spring will either be bitter or it'll be sweet, but it's never both. In everything else, it's either this or that. It's either a boy or it's a girl. It's not a boy who wants to be a girl. It's not a girl who wants to be a boy. It is what it is.

Enter Satan, who blurs the lines. If we blur the lines, I can move into another side undetected. If I have an official line of demarcation, the moment I cross that line you knew I crossed it. But if I can blur the line, then I can move with impunity to any side I want, and you will not know I was there until the damage has been done.

If a spring has bitter water, the water is bitter. If the spring has sweet water, then it's sweet, but a spring cannot put out both at any time. Why? It doesn't have a brain so it doesn't have a choice. That's why James said, "Out of the same mouth flows bitter and sweet." Your mouth has a choice. Because it has a choice, whatever influences it at that time is what comes out. You're having a good day and proclaim, "God is so good! He's my Redeemer! He's my Light! He's my Shepherd! He's my Strong Tower! Glory to God! He's my Bright and Morning Star!" Then you have a bad day. You get a distressing phone call on the way to work. All of a sudden, "I don't understand why God's forsaken me. I don't know why. Doesn't He love me? I've been tithing and serving and giving and He doesn't care about me!" How did blessing and curse come out of the same mouth? How do you leave church 10 feet tall and bulletproof and by Monday, if you had a can, you'd kick it?

It can't be both. God knows that if I'm going to put my blessing on you, then I have to get you to understand you're not cursed. Cursed and blessing can't operate at the same time. If it can't operate at the same time, I have to now bring you into right standing.

Facebook is not a friend to some of you. Matter of fact, some of you should shut your Facebook page down and stay off until you can stop cussing. It's so bizarre how someone can post "I went to church today!" immediately followed by "@#$%&!" Really? How does that same mouth profess God? I don't know how that's possible. My God is the same every day. When I come to church, I come to get filled up. But I don't stay full from church service to church service. I get emptied out during the week. Then Wednesday comes and I get filled up again and that holds me over to Sunday. I'm constantly pouring out. This is why when I get an opportunity to praise with my brothers and sisters, this isn't the only time that I praise. Sometimes I've got to throw a party all by myself. Those are some of the best parties I've ever been to.

When you know you're blessed, it's hard to think like a cursed person. So many people think that they are cursed. How do I know that? Because they are constantly wondering why they go through what they go through. "I don't understand why I'm struggling with my money and my health. I've been fighting for my children's health. I've been fighting for my finances." When you think that way, you are making it clear that you do not believe God is your supply and your provider. When you start saying God won't do thus-and-so and something hasn't happened that you wish would, and so-and-so is this way, and you're sick with this and that, you give more credence to the manifestation of the curse. There are manifestations of the blessing.

Someone says, "Oh wow, you have a brand new car; that's such a blessing." No, it's not. The car, the stuff, the things are not what's important. The Giver is important. If I have a relationship with my God, then He has promised me He'd take care of me. Will I be able to wash myself in gold nuggets? Obviously that's a little bit much. Of course, some of these people on TV would have you believe that's what God wants you to do. That's not true, but God does want me to have a full supply. He wants me to be able to supply for my children. He wants me to be able to send them to college. He wants me to be able to take care of them. He wants my family to be able to be in a home that we own.

One of the three promises that God gave Abraham was, "I will give you a land." If we receive the promise of the spirit through faith, if that's supposed to come upon you, what promise is He talking about? The promise that He made to Abraham. He said, "I will make your name great. I will give you land that you did not do anything for. I'll give it to you." We should have the ability to understand that God wants us to be blessed so we can be a blessing! You can't help anybody into what you don't have. If you've never owned a home before, don't talk to me about how to buy one. It doesn't make any kind of sense.

You've gotten to a place where you understand how the curse manifests. "Well, I'm struggling with sickness in my body." That's not the curse, that's the manifestation of the curse. You can learn how to manifest the curse in your life. Did you ever meet somebody that everything they say is negative? You see them coming into church and you head the other direction. You don't want to ask them, "Hey! How are you doing?" You already know they'll say, "Oh, my dog... he ain't doing so hot, and my life..." You're thinking, "Could you ever just say I'm doing good, God is on the throne, I'm blessed and highly favored?"

Remember when Job said, "The thing I fear the most has come upon me" (Job 3:25). How does the thing you don't want to happen occur so much in your life? Many of you are like, "If I didn't have bad luck I'd have no luck at all." That's your problem. I don't have any luck, period. I don't have bad luck, I don't have good luck. I have God! People want to play with luck through the lottery, through the casino. You then begin to speak like a person who needs luck. Now when you speak like that sort of person, you begin to manifest that which only luck can take or bring. You then relinquish control of the spigot to something other than you, as if God didn't die for you. Or maybe on Monday He did, but Tuesday He didn't. Maybe on Wednesday He did but Thursday He didn't. It's bitter and sweet coming out of the same spring. It becomes curse and blessing and you're choking out your seed. Why plant one thing that kills and chokes out the other? One day you're talking about how good God is, and the next day you're saying, "I can't get through what just happened to me." How do we flip-flop back and forth? It's because you don't know that the whole reason He said, "I have to get the curse off of you so I can put just the blessing on you."

His Word didn't say that He would put both on you or give you access to promises every once in a while. Some of you have a doctrinal problem. You think that God is in no way, shape, or form able to bless you. You think that God does not care about your health, the health of your children, your prosperity, your supply, your home, or you being able to send your children to college without putting them into so much debt that they'll have to work their way through.

You sent them to college for the purpose of increasing their knowledge so that they can hopefully aspire to a higher level than you. But when you sent them and they didn't have money, they acquired higher debt that is the equivalent of what you tried to get them into. But now they lose it, however, because Satan robs them and they end up paying this money for the rest of their lives for an education that was going to better their life. Why is it so hard for you to think God wants you to have the money to send your kids to college? Why is it so difficult to think that God wants you to own land and homes? He said, "I'll give you vineyards that you didn't plant." It's a doctrinal problem. You're approaching your situations with the thought that God is not there and doesn't care.

My hat's off to all the single mothers who've had to raise children because you had to be mom and dad, and you've done an excellent job at that because it's hard to do. But I believe that men should be in their children's lives. Men are important, fathers are important to their children. There's something about a kid who thinks their daddy can beat up everybody. You know some kids that you wanted to knock upside the head, but something in them just says, "I'm all right. I can take you, and if I can't take you my daddy can." There is a confidence and almost a cockiness about them. A child says, "My daddy is bigger than your daddy." Now if your daddy is 3'2" and 60 pounds soaking wet, he'd better know kung fu or something.

My Daddy is definitely bigger. So how come we lack the confidence to say that, to be that, to live that? It's because we still haven't figured out what it means when the curse is truly removed from our life. Did you ever hear somebody say, "I just can't catch a break. If it ain't one thing, it's another. I'm caught between a rock and a hard place." How do we ever move beyond that to the place where we realize that yes, many are the afflictions of the righteous, but the Bible says that God will deliver them out of them all (see Psalm 34:19). All of them. Everything that comes my direction that is not of God, He will deliver me out of. The Bible says, "Cast not away therefore your confidence for it has great recompense of reward" (Hebrews 10:35). In other words, you can't let your confidence towards God be taken away from you. If it's taken away from you, what do you have to fight with? If your Daddy truly isn't bigger, then what do you have from this point forward to look forward to?

God said, "Let Me get you out of the curse and let me put My blessing on you so you can experience what Abraham experienced." When the blessing's in operation, it will manifest in your life. The car isn't blessed, I am. The house isn't blessed, I am. When things come into my life, when I needed that something and it showed up right on time, the Bible says, "Every good and perfect gift comes from above" (James 1:17). If every good and perfect gift came from Him, then it is not the gift that's the blessing. They're just manifestations. It's you who are blessed and begin to produce blessings. If you ever start thinking that the car is blessed, then don't you ever drive another car again. If the car is blessed, you'd better stay in it. You'd better figure out how to work from inside of that car, figure out how to do everything in the car. But you know that doesn't make sense. All that is, is mere stuff.

Why would God put His blessing on stuff? That makes people materialistic. They think that he who dies with the most toys wins. It's not true. You are already blessed. He said when you believe in Jesus, you become blessed with faithful Abraham. He says now the blessing of Abraham will come upon the Gentiles. The blessing puts you in a position where you don't have to act or function like someone who is cursed. If you cannot find 24 hours in a 7-day period of time to love on your spouse, to spend with your children, you are toiling and you're not walking in the blessing. That's not my opinion. I love to work, I enjoy work. I could work seven days a week and be fine with it. That's just me personally. What I'm quoting to you is from God's Word. The challenge becomes when you are living unto God, you are professing that God is your supply. Yet, you work yourself to where you violate natural law and His spiritual law, then you wonder why you struggle.

Hebrews 3:18-19; 4:1-11 (NASB)
"And to whom did He swear that they would not enter His rest, but to those who were disobedient? So we see that they were not able to enter because of unbelief...Therefore, let us fear if, while a promise remains of entering His rest, any one of you may seem to have come short of it. For indeed we have had good news preached to us, just as they also; but the word they heard did not profit them, because it was not united by faith in those who heard. For we who have believed enter that rest, just as He has said, 'As I swore in My wrath, They shall not enter My rest,' although His works were finished from the foundation of the world. For He has said somewhere concerning the seventh day: 'And God rested on the seventh day from all His works'; and again in this passage, 'They shall not enter My rest.' Therefore, since it remains for some to enter it, and those who formerly had good news preached to them

failed to enter because of disobedience, He again fixes a certain day, 'Today,' saying through David after so long a time just as has been said before, 'Today if you hear His voice, Do not harden your hearts.' For if Joshua had given them rest, He would not have spoken of another day after that. So there remains a Sabbath rest for the people of God. For the one who has entered His rest has himself also rested from his works, as God did from His. Therefore let us be diligent to enter that rest, so that no one will fall, through following the same example of disobedience."

He's talking about the Sabbath. Does the Bible tell us we're supposed to have a Sabbath? Yes, it's one of the Ten Commandments. So if the Sabbath was concerning Joshua, it would not have been spoken after Joshua. It would have been done away with. But because it was still spoken, that means there still is a rest. God rested from his works. God made the Earth in six days and on the seventh day He rested. He didn't go back to work on the eighth. He was done. Do you think that on the sixth day he was like, "Phew! Child, I'm tired! All this moving mountains and water—this is exhausting." No, God spoke it all into existence. He said it, it happened. When He told the water to separate, the water said, "Oh, okay," and separated. There's a lyric in the song *My Redeemer Lives* by Nicole. C Mullen that reads, "Who told the ocean it could only come this far?" He said it, and it happened. For Him to rest on the seventh day was purely to demonstrate for you what was about to come.

The reason God changed Abram's name to Abraham is because "Abraham" means "Father of many nations." So every time Abraham heard his name, he heard "Father of many nations." God said, "I made a promise to Abraham and I need Abraham to stop acting like he's not blessed. So the way I'm going to get Abraham to be clear about what I've done for him is, I'm going to change his name. Every time somebody says, 'Yo, Abraham!' he hears, 'Father of many nations.' Every time he thinks about his own name, he hears 'Father of many nations.' " Now all of a sudden "faith cometh by hearing and hearing by the Word of God" (see Romans 10:17). So he keeps hearing, "Father of many nations." It helps him to stay on the promise.

Now God says, "Okay, I've done it all. Now I'm going to rest on the seventh day because I want my children to know that every time they rest, this was not for Me. I did it for them." It was to teach you something. Every time you see a Sabbath, you are thumbing your nose at Satan. Every time I go onto my Sabbath—It doesn't matter what day. I know some people who are sticklers about the day, but to me it doesn't matter what day. Mine happens to be Monday.

Now, do you think my phone stops ringing on Monday? Do you think all the problems go away on Monday? Don't you think I sit there and Satan goes, "You know if you don't deal with this today, it's going to be twice as bad tomorrow. If you don't do this today, you might miss something." One of the biggest fears that seems to have entered into today's society is the fear of missing out. It's not new. Why do you think children won't go to sleep? Fear of missing out. They believe that somehow after they go to sleep, nymphs come out of the walls and their parents have some huge party that they're not privy to. It's the fear of missing out.

Adults have gotten to a place where they're like, "I can't take that day off. What if I miss out? Pastor, you don't understand; I need the money. I can't take the day off. I can't go to church, I have to work on Sunday." And Satan's laughing all the way to the bank. He's saying, "See? They can't rest." The Lord said the reason they couldn't enter wasn't because Satan attacked them, it's because what they heard couldn't be mixed with faith. They couldn't get their heads around the idea that God was going to give them rest. They couldn't believe that there would come a moment, a time, when they don't have to work themselves to death to get what God has for them. There would come a time that I would actually be walking in the Sabbath rest that comes for the believer today. It is not just me working that produces it, but it's the fact the blessing is on my life that things begin to happen just because God loves me. Now I don't have to toil in order to get it. All I have to do is mix what I've heard with faith.

God said there comes a sabbath rest that remaineth (see Hebrews 4:9). What do you think that is? God didn't go back to work on the eighth day. So resting on the seventh was a demonstration to teach you that every week He's going to remind you that there comes rest. When the rest happens, all you're really acknowledging is that there's really coming another rest when you won't go back to work. The sabbath, that day of rest, is the way you know you're not in toil. The worst altercation I ever had with my ex-wife that turned physical against me was over the sabbath. I have never been fought harder on anything like I did the sabbath (which I had been working to get a sabbath for a long time). The sabbath is your way of saying, "I will not be moved."

Here's what I can assure you of. Every time I took my sabbath, the problems were still there. While I was resting, relaxing, and enjoying the things I wanted to do as unto the Lord, problems were still there. But I was letting Satan know that although you have created problems, your problems will not control me. And I was letting God know that I trusted Him enough, come what may. So as the Sabbath rolled around every single week, it was teaching me to let it go. The Martha in you can rise up and all of a sudden you're like, "Tell Mary to go do some work!" Jesus said, "She chose what was important." Work is fine, I love work. If you don't work, you'll be in the street. Everybody should work. I detest a person who refuses to work. They don't make 'em like they used to. Get four hours of work out of some people and they're done.

The Lord said they couldn't get into the rest aspect because they couldn't take what they heard and mix it with faith. They couldn't believe that while they're resting, God is still moving. Somewhere in the nature of a person, their predilection is to believe they are God. I know you don't want to admit that because it sounds blasphemous (and it is) but the truth remains that in most people this thought always seems to pop up when tragedy hits. When something goes wrong, the first thing you say is, "I made this mistake and I did this." What if Satan did it? What if he just threw it at you? I was just minding my own business and wham! No, the first thing you say is, "It's my fault," because you're God. Or, the next thing you do is to say, "I have to fix it."

So now I've got to get ten jobs. Now my family doesn't see me anymore. Now I'm so tired when I come home that all I do is sleep. The kids are tugging at the bed sheet. "Mommy! Mommy!" You yell back, "What!?" "…Nothing." But they did want something; they wanted you. But you've entered into toiling because you think you have to fix the problem because you're God.

They couldn't mix it with faith, they couldn't get behind it and believe there's coming a moment in time where Jesus will come and He would pay the price. Then the curse will be lifted and the blessing will be placed. When I'm blessed, I don't have to toil. I don't have to hurt myself. I don't have to work myself to death to the place where I've got money longer than train smoke, but I'll never live to spend it. I've violated all the natural laws and the spiritual laws. God said the reason they couldn't enter was because they couldn't mix it with faith.

What we begin to see is that God says, "I want them to enter into My rest." Let me say it this way: the type of rest that I have, I don't have to keep going back to work. I can come to church and I don't have to think about work while I'm there. I can receive whatever God has for me. I can go out to dinner with my family and not be looking at my watch because I have a report due tomorrow morning. I can go on a date with my husband or wife and I don't have to be like, "Oh my God, I still have stuff that I took home and I have to get it done!" He said, "I'm trying to help you understand that if you are in Me, there's a rest that comes with Me. The reason the rest comes with Me, with Me, help showed up."

Did you ever have a paint and pizza party, or you have people over to help you move and promise them food? They show up more for the food than they do for the work. Do you think God is like that? When He shows up, He's there for other stuff that you don't realize. The Bible says He never sleeps. If He never sleeps, then there's no sense in both of us being up all night long. You're worrying about how this is going to work or how that is going to happen. He says, "All I want you to do is enter into My rest." He said when you have a sabbath, it's not about obligation. It's not even about the law. It's about, "Do you trust Me enough to put it down and to give Me a tithe of your week?"

People think tithe is just about money; it's not. It's about, "Hey, how do I get a tenth of your week? How do I get a tenth of your time?" You can show up and soak up our air conditioning and enjoy all the stuff that we do and all the music and all the things that happen around here, but you don't think it's important for you to put your time in. "Well, Pastor, I'll just put a little more money in because I ain't tryin' to—" What do you mean you ain't trying to? God wants all of you!

When I have a sabbath, I am literally entering into His rest. It is my acknowledgement that His rest even exists. It's my acknowledgment that says I'm not going to work myself to death. What is it that manifests in my life if I die prematurely? It's a curse. The curse of not having anything, the curse of working your fingers to the bone twelve hours a day, six to seven days a week, and you still don't have anything left. It's like putting money into a bag with holes in it (see Haggai 1:6) and you're trying to figure out why you keep working so hard but don't have anything? It becomes toil and that's a curse. It is a curse to have to work excessively to have nothing. It's a curse for you to die and everybody has to come together for a car wash to put you in the ground.

God says, "I want you to enter into My rest. I want to take the curse off of your life and I'm going to put a blessing on that when I bless your life, the fruit from that blessing will manifest into the world.

Whatever it is you need, I want you to depend on Me so when that seventh day comes around and the sabbath is here, you're able to push it to the side and say, 'You know what? It's going to be here then.' " Because my God is well able and if I trust in Him, I know He's got my back. So I look towards the hills to where my help comes from. I don't care about the stuff, I don't care about the things. They can have it all. Just don't take God's anointing from off my neck.

It's about God. He wants you to be able to call your boss and say, "Yeah, I know I was working but I can't do that anymore." "Well, we're going to have to let you go." "Well then, thank God I have One who will never let me go. So if you do let me go, I would advise you of something. It is quite possible that the only reason your company is still around is because of me."

I know some of you think that's just ridiculous. Ask Potiphar about Joseph. When Joseph showed up, Potiphar started prospering. The blessing wasn't on Potiphar. Joseph didn't have anything. Joseph was a slave. When you can write an entire business being a slave just because you showed up, you have to understand God gave you dominion while you were naked in the garden. Adam and Eve didn't have a thing, but God gave them dominion in the midst of the garden. They had nothing and they were naked. They didn't have any Giorgio Armani, no Givenchy, or Prada. They were naked with dominion. Wherever Joseph showed up, that country prospered. Don't think I'm telling you something that's heretical. There are some of you that the place where you work is still around because you are there.

When we moved into our first building in Peoria, AZ, I spoke to the owner and said, "If you put us in here, this plaza will start filling up." When we moved in there, there was a barbershop and a clothing store and that was it. But after we moved in, businesses started coming in. Now the owner made some terrible decisions and lost some of those businesses, but it started to fill up as soon as we moved in. I told her that's what would happen.

I'm blessed to be a blessing and God said, "I will bless those that bless you." So that means if you do right by me, God will bless you because the blessing is on me. If the blessing is on me, then all you have to recognize is if you treat me right, you will make it. But if you've got the audacity to be on the phone and tell me I can't have Sundays off and you're going to fire me? Bye! You will receive by how you deal.

The Bible talks about fallow ground. It says you should rotate your crops and then on one year let your ground lay fallow, which means don't do anything with it, just leave it alone. The reason for that is to allow the ground to recover. Then on the sixth year, stock up so you'll have enough to take care of you through the fallow year. When you get through the fallow, then start back into the process again.

Some of you may know of George Washington Carver, the peanut man. If you don't know the history, let me help you. The farmers were planting so much cotton in rotation that they had depleted the soil. Carver figured out that if they rotated in some peanuts, the peanut crop would actually replenish the ground so they could go back into their cycle of harvest for cotton. That's how peanuts became so popular. Later, he came up with many other uses for peanuts. His premise was that with continual functioning of the cotton crop, it depleted the soil. When the ground became depleted, the crop began to suffer.

Carver realized that if the ground doesn't have what it needs, it can no longer produce. If you don't think it's important for you to be filled when you come to church, when you think it's okay to stay home, "I don't need a sabbath day. I don't need to be in the Lord's house," when you don't think it's important to replenish and you let yourself lay fallow, that's why you're struggling right now.

It's easy to mix faith when you're rested. It's hard to mix faith when you have been going and going and going... that's why they tell you to never make an important decision when you're exhausted because you'll make it out of your emotions. You wonder why you don't see the manifestations in your life; it's because you haven't found the time to lay fallow. You haven't found the time to say, "You know what? I know I've been working on this cotton crop for the last six days, but on the seventh day I'm going to get me some peanuts."

I'm not going to allow myself to get caught in this rut. I'm going to stop everything I'm doing, I'm going to teach my children to stop everything they're doing, and I'm going to live my life as unto God knowing that when I show up, God is very much with me and that everywhere I go, He is there. If I am blessed then when I show up, wherever I show up, has also become blessed. When I go to negotiate, guess what? I'm blessed. You want to do right by me? You'll be blessed. You want to do me wrong? I wouldn't advise that. The Lord said, "I will bless those that bless you and curse those that curse you" (see Genesis 12:3).

Do you really believe that? When people do me wrong, my wife will tell you I'm genuinely concerned for them. I'm dumb enough to believe the Word. You want to stand against me, attack me, take money from me, try to rob me, try to hurt me, try to steal from me, talk bad about me? Are you crazy? Those that curse me, God will curse! I don't have to fight this battle; the battle is not mine. The battle is the Lord's! I don't have to fight with you! He didn't say that's only for the pastor. He said that's for every single one of you that the blessing of Abraham might come upon the Gentile.

Now you're wondering why you're doing things in the natural, you're planting your cotton crop but it just isn't producing. It's because you—the ground it's being planted in—has lost all its nutrients. You have nothing left. "Pastor, I'm just maintaining. The struggle is real! I'm just getting by, Pastor. You don't understand. It's hard in the street." It's not hard in the street; it's hard in you because you haven't learned that there are spiritual principles at work.

If supernatural power could be given through spiritual things, why cannot supernatural wealth be given through spiritual things? Why do you think it's not important for you to invest in you, that fallow ground, for you to recover? Spend some time with God. Here's an idea: study your Bible. It's not just enough to take a day off and sleep all the way through it. Take what you would have given to Satan and give it to God.

Remember in the sixth year they stored up enough so that in the seventh year they didn't have to do anything? Did you know that the Jewish culture has a 24-hour sabbath from Friday sundown to sundown on Saturday? They even cook their meals on Friday before the sabbath starts so they don't have to cook on the sabbath. The only thing that breaks their sabbath is an emergency, like if their child gets sick or something like that. You have to deal with that. You can't say, "Little Jimmy, wait until tomorrow." But if it's not an emergency, they have enough forethought to stock up on the sixth day to where they don't have to do it on the seventh day. That's how important it is for them.

Yet, when I say to you, "Do you have a day of rest?" Your response might be "Well you know, Pastor, we go to church on Sunday morning but Sunday night I have to do the laundry, get the kids ready for school the next day..." They always have school the next day. They've been having school on Monday as long as I've been going to school. You knew on Friday that Monday was coming. This is what people do. At what point do you stop and say, "I'm going to give this to God"? Because when you won't give it to Him, you're saying He's not going to take care of it so you're going to have to do it yourself.

I guarantee you that you're going to be fought on this. Kids are going to fight you on it, even your dog's going to fight you on it. That's what's going to trip you up when your dog looks you in the face and goes, "I ain't trying to take off today!" But when you do it by faith, you will see much begin to change. What happens is, you take it off of your shoulders and roll your cares onto the Lord, and you learn how to act like He acts. He didn't take the rest because He needed it.

Some of you are like, "I don't need a day off. I'm good." Yeah, you're good today. I remember when I was younger I could eat a pizza as big as a wagon wheel. Today, I'd be up all night long (and not for any spiritual activity either). I'd be having all kinds of stupid dreams. You learn as you get a little older, you can't do what you used to. All that hot sauce and peppers and sausage... you learn you have to do some things a little differently. I'm not trying to let my words trip me up, but some of you know what I'm talking about.

I challenge you to realize that while you may not be paying the price for it now (which you really are, but you may not know it), take the time to figure it out. It doesn't matter what day it is, but you need to figure out how to give those 24 hours of your life over to God. Rest and pray with your family, study, and do things that build up your fallow ground so the next day you are rejuvenated and refreshed.

I'm going to give you the answer real quick to where I was going. When the Lord was talking about the believer's rest, here's what He was talking about. Yes, we understand sabbath as we rest on the seventh and go back to work on the first. However, He was saying that there's coming a time where, as a believer, you'll never have to go back to work. This was a dispensation of grace. It wasn't really that you don't have to work, sit on your butt, and do nothing. That's not what He's talking about. He's saying the days of you having to toil are over.

After Jesus died on the cross, you don't have to toil anymore. There are things that come to you because you're His child. There are things that begin to move in your life because He's your God. He said, "I will make you my people and I will be your God" (Exodus 6:7). Now I have a relationship that causes me not to have to toil because there's a difference between work and toil. Work you have to do, toil you don't. Entering into the believer's rest is letting you know you will no longer have to strive and stretch and reach for what I'm going to give you. That's why He said after David, they're still talking about this rest, so it couldn't be Joshua leading them into the Promised Land. It had to be something else. Jesus died for you so you have the privilege of not having to strive for everything in your life. Now you can rest.

Rest is important. Change your perspective. In my rest times, that's when God speaks to me the most. Things I couldn't figure out and get an answer to, I understand more clearly when I get to a place of rest.

Have you ever wondered why you get your greatest revelations when you're in the shower? It's because you're alone and insulated and isolated. That's it! Now He can talk to you. He's like, "I got you like I got Adam. I've got you buck naked and attentive. Now let's talk a little bit!" You might laugh, but it's true.

Putting God First

1 Samuel 6:1-9 (KJV)

"And the ark of the LORD was in the country of the Philistines seven months. And the Philistines called for the priests and the diviners, saying, What shall we do to the ark of the LORD? Tell us in what way we shall send it to its place. And they said, If ye send away the ark of the God of Israel, send it not empty; but in any wise return him a trespass offering: then ye shall be healed, and it shall be known to you why his hand is not removed from you. Then said they, What shall be the trespass offering which we shall return to him? They answered, Five golden emrods, and five golden mice, according to the number of the lords of the Philistines: for one plague was on you all, and on your lords. Wherefore ye shall make images of your emrods, and images of your mice that mar the land; and ye shall give glory unto the God of Israel. Peradventure he will lighten his hand from you, and from your gods, and from your land. Why, then, do ye harden your hearts, as the Egyptians and Pharaoh hardened their hearts? When he had wrought wonderfully among them, did they not let the people go, and they departed? Now, therefore, make a new cart, and take two milch kine, on which there hath come no yoke, and tie the kine to the cart, and bring their calves home from them. And take the ark of the LORD, and lay it upon the cart; and put the jewels of gold, which ye return him for a trespass offering, in a coffer by the side of it; and send it away, that it may go. And see, if it goeth up by the way of his own coast to Bethshemesh, then he hath done us this great evil: but if not, then we shall know that it is not his hand that smote us; it was a chance that happened to us."

It is interesting to see that when the Philistines captured the ark, great plagues started to come upon them. They had moved the ark into the house of Dagon, which was their god, and put the ark next to it. It was a huge statue. When they came back the next day, Dagon was lying prostrate before the ark, almost as if someone had smacked him in the back of his head. The Philistines saw Dagon lying on the ground and assumed maybe he fell, and they put him back up. When they came back the next day, God had not only knocked Dagon down, but He had cut off his head and his hands.

They were doing all right until they captured the ark. Now all of a sudden, everywhere they moved it, calamity seemed to fall upon their lives. So then, the Philistines decided they were going to send the ark back from where it came because they had nothing but bad luck. I use the word "luck" intentionally because the Bible says "chance," which some of you like to play with (i.e., fortunes, horoscopes, casinos, etc.). They're trying to figure out if all the stuff going on in their lives is luck or has the God of Israel gone out against them. Not knowing what to do, they went to their priests and diviners who told them, "Here's what you do. You get two milk cows [there's a difference between oxen that pull and a milk cow] that have never been yoked up before, and you find two that have just had some babies. Put the babies in the barn and yoke them to a cart. Put the ark on it; make an offering of emrods [hemorrhoids] and mice." (They made images of hemorrhoids because that's what God struck them with. That's low! I mean you want to fight dirty, that's fighting dirty.) Then they made graven images of mice—because a plague of mice had come—and put them in a coffer, or box, next to the ark.

The priests then said, "Here's what will happen; these milk cows will either run to their children because that's instinctively what they do, or they'll carry this thing back to the children of Israel. But most likely if it's not God, they'll go back to their children because that's what they would naturally and intuitively do." So they did all of that. They set it all up, loaded it up, let them puppies go, and they made a beeline. They said, "Forget the kids!" So they began to realize that God was in it.

The thing about this whole issue is that they took the ark by force. Here it is that God is now forcing them to give it back. There have been things that have truly been taken from you and oftentimes you look for other people in order to replenish what someone else had stolen not realizing that God can make them give it back.

I'll give you a good example. Sometimes when you have a bad relationship with somebody, you make the next relationship pay for what the previous one did. Someone stole from you and now you're borrowing from somebody else. You do that because you don't necessarily understand how God works. Let me give you the definition of "protocol"; It's *"the official procedure, system or rules of governing affairs of state or diplomatic occasions; a form of ceremony and etiquette observed by diplomats in heads of state; a set of conventional principles and expectations that are considered binding on any person who is a member of a particular group."*

Here, they have decided they're going to send the ark back and they send it to a town called Bethshemesh. When the ark gets there, the townspeople notice the ark coming by itself, being pulled by some cows. They run to the ark, check it out to see what's going on, look inside of it, and God kills thousands of them.

1 Samuel 6:20-21 (KJV)
"And the men of Bethshemesh said, Who is able to stand before this holy LORD God? and to whom shall he go up from us? And they sent messengers to the inhabitants of Kirjathjearim, saying, The Philistines have brought again the ark of the LORD; come ye down, and fetch it up to you."

Here the ark (the presence of God, the physical embodiment of His physical presence) is now a curse to the Philistines, so they get rid of it and send it back to the children of Israel. They get it, and it's a curse to them. So they're wondering who in the world is capable of standing before God? They say, "It seems like even though we're being told and we've been raised to know that we are the chosen people, when we saw the presence of God coming back, we were super excited because the blessing had come back into our lives. We ran to it, and all we did was open and look in it and thousands are now dead. Who is able to stand? It's one thing to say we're a blessed people. It's one thing to say that this ark is so important to us, but when we are still dying, who's able to deal with this thing?" It sends a signal that it may very well be a problem.

> 2 Samuel 6:5-11 (KJV)
> *"And David and all the house of Israel played before the Lord on all manner of instruments made of fir wood, even on harps, and on psalteries, and on timbrels, and on cornets, and on cymbals. And when they came to Nachon's threshing floor, Uzzah put forth his hand to the ark of God, and took hold of it; for the oxen shook it. And the anger of the LORD was kindled against Uzzah; and God smote him there for his error; and there he died by the ark of God. And David was displeased, because the LORD had made a breach upon Uzzah: and he called the name of the place Perezuzzah to this day. And David was afraid of the LORD that day, and said, How shall the ark of the LORD come to me? So David would not remove the ark of the LORD unto him into the city of David; but David carried it aside into the house of Obededom the Gittite. And the ark of the LORD continued in the house of Obededom, the Gittite, three months: and the LORD blessed Obededom, and all his household."*

There's a saying that says one man's trash is another man's treasure. David is displeased, but there's a challenge here. As the ark is being moved on the cart, the cart hits a rocky road and it begins to vibrate as if it's going to fall off. Uzzah reaches up his hand to touch the ark in order to keep it from falling. The anger of the Lord was kindled against him, and God struck him dead. Now David is upset because in his head, God breached Uzzah. The truth of the matter is that Uzzah breached God.

I think it's important to understand that when you don't recognize something for what it is, it often can seem to you to be something very different. For example, Esau who had the blessing on his life, but yet sold it for some stew, then said, "What good is it to me to live with a blessing and then die?" This gives you the understanding that he did not perceive or see the value of what was going on with the blessing. Here's my challenge: as the ark leaves the Philistines, they place it on the cart and none of them were struck dead. The cart shows up, they look inside, and thousands are struck dead. The cart's being moved, Uzzah reaches up trying to help God out, but he's struck dead. Now they move it into Obededom's house because David's afraid of it.

If you study Obededom, you'll find that many theologians believe that he had 60 to 70 servants, so he was a pretty well-to-do individual. Can you imagine what that must have been like to have the ark in your house, and all of a sudden, your cows and your children are prospering like crazy? Everything concerning your household begins to be blessed because God is blessing it. This is the same thing that seemed to be a curse for other people, causing them to wonder why they're having such a struggle and why their luck is so bad. All of the things they experienced were very different when the ark was moved in the house of Obededom. Now David gets wind of this and hears about Obededom being blessed and says, "We've got to go down there and get that thing!" You know you're blessed when the president shows up at your house to see what's really going on!

We tend not to want what we don't understand. When they said, "Come get this thing," David saw Uzzah die and wanted to get rid of it immediately. Nobody thought to ask if there was a protocol. What we don't understand, we tend to dismiss as if it's not important. When David sees that Obededom's house is blessed, he's like, "We've got to go get this. Maybe God's changed His mind. Maybe His anger has subsided. Maybe it took Him three months to get over the fact that the Philistines had it."

The truth of the matter is procedure and protocol are not the same. I can come up with procedure in order to figure out how to accomplish something, but procedure will take *me* into account. What's *my* fastest way to get something done? What's *my* easiest way to get it done? When I give somebody a procedure on how to do something, oftentimes they take it and twist it into what works for them. In their head they say, "As long as we got to the same place, what does it matter?" Similarly, when we deal with God, we tend to take what He gives us and try to manipulate it into something that works for us. We begin to modify the things that really are not procedure, they're protocol. There is no procedure with God, there's protocol with Him. Procedure brings us down to a level of a lower existence. When you deal with protocol, you're dealing with diplomats, with a higher level of people. Aristocracy and theocracy brings about protocol; it says the way you deal with me is the way I deal with you.

We often struggle in relationships because we do not realize that proximity brings familiarity. When you first meet someone, you want to know what her favorite color was. You ask all the exploratory questions: What's your favorite kind of music? What's your favorite flower? What's your sign? (Stop sign!) There comes a point where you don't care anymore what her favorite flowers are because you're not buying them anyway. Because of familiarity, we begin to walk away from things.

Now when you were at home by yourself before she was your wife and you wanted a wife, you spent a lot of time thinking about how you could come up with a wonderful date and some creative ideas and things you could do. You thought to bring flowers, candy, etc., and you came up with elaborate concocted schemes of how you would woo her, based on protocol. Then, after you got her, now it's all about procedure. "The restaurant is 30 minutes that way, can't we find one that's 5 minutes this way? That saves us time, and I can get back and watch the game." You have relegated protocol down to procedure.

There's a saying, "You never miss the water till the well runs dry." Also, "Absence makes the heart grow fonder." Both of these sayings are based on the premise that when you relegate protocol to procedure, you become too familiar. When you begin to look at relationship as a series of decisions, checkpoints, things to do, you have lost the real nature of the relationship. "I don't need to take her out to the finest restaurant, the fast-food place will do. She gets fed, she's no longer hungry, and we can get this over with." When you're concerned with what you think, all of a sudden you lose sight of what they think. You should be asking yourself, "What's his/her favorite meal? What's his/her favorite thing?" When you put yourself out there to do what the other wants, you have protocol in the relationship.

Here's another example: You come to church, and if the pastor doesn't call you back then you're mad. However, if your boyfriend doesn't call you back, and he's sleeping around, some of you would take him back. You don't get a return phone call from the church, you think nobody cares and you're gone. That's protocol.

David realizes that in order to bring this ark back home, he has to get the Levites together. Finally, they have reached a place where they have now followed what God told them to do. God said if you're going to move the ark, it's supposed to be carried—not by a cart, but by rods through gold rings and carried by the Levites. God had given them a way in which to deal with Him, but the Philistines did not know that. Therefore, they were not held accountable for what they did not know.

Protocol is based only on a specific group of people who belong to that group. If I'm not from your country, I may not understand your culture. If I don't understand your culture, I can offend someone. But if you are from that country you are expected to know protocol. So here come the Philistines. They're picking up the ark, throwing it on a cart, and nothing happens to them. God gets among His chosen people and He starts striking out. They have become so familiar that they forgot there was protocol. They deal with God based on their curiosity. "How dare you look inside when you know you're not supposed to?" But they think it's okay because they relegated protocol down to procedure and said, "I'll do it anyway because it's okay. It's no big deal. It's only the presence of God," and the blessing of God literally is moving throughout the country. It is cursing people because they don't know how to deal with God, but it should be a blessing. They relegated God down to their own understanding, but He said, "I'm the God who changes not." If He's this way before, He's this way tomorrow, and He doesn't change based on your desire to move Him into a different place. He doesn't change because we want Him to be different. He doesn't change because we've gotten smarter about this world and we figure if He knew what we knew, He'd change. He does not!

So many people want a key to deal with God. "Just tell me what I have to do, Pastor. Give me the procedure." There is none, there's protocol. David gets the Levites in and every seven paces they take, they make a sacrifice. Now, all of a sudden they're getting it together. They're doing it the way God told them to do it. They make it all the way to the city of David. Go figure.

2 Samuel 6:16-23 (KJV)
"And as the ark of the LORD came into the city of David, Michal, Saul's daughter looked through a window, and saw King David leaping and dancing before the LORD; and she despised him in her heart. And they brought in the ark of the LORD, and set it in its place, in the midst of the tabernacle that David had pitched for it; and David offered burnt offerings and peace offerings before the LORD. And as soon as David had made an end of offering burnt offerings and peace offerings, he blessed the people in the name of the LORD of hosts. And he dealt among all the people, even among the whole multitude of Israel, as well to the women as men, to everyone a cake of bread, and a good piece of flesh, and a flagon

of wine. So all the people departed everyone to his house. Then David returned to bless his household. And Michal, the daughter of Saul, came out to meet David, and said, How glorious was the king of Israel today, who uncovered himself to day in the eyes of the handmaids of his servants, as one of the vain fellows shamelessly uncovereth himself! And David said unto Michal, It was before the LORD, which chose me before thy father, and before all his house, to appoint me ruler over the people of the LORD, over Israel; therefore will I play before the LORD. And I will yet be more vile than thus, and will be base in mine own sight; and of the maidservants whom thou hast spoken of, of them shall I be had in honor. Therefore, Michal, the daughter of Saul, had no child unto the day of her death."

David's not dancing naked, he just stripped down of all his priestly robes. He's dancing in his garments as if he was a pauper, and Michal is upset because in her mind he's royalty. That's why he said, "I can get more vile than this." The word "vile" here doesn't mean evil, it means *a lack of vanity.* He didn't care how people saw him, because before the Lord he was nothing. The servants were to honor him, but when he went before God, he was as one of them. That's why he said, "I'll abase myself." "Abase" means *to bring yourself to a low position, to shrink back in your importance.* Michal is the daughter of Saul. Saul had such a bad attitude that he thought he was above everything and everyone, and we see how that worked out for him. Here, Michal is obviously of that same school of thought. She's laughing and despising David because he's dancing mightily before God.

God hasn't done anything to David yet, He just showed up. He hasn't had time. Three months at Obededom's house and all of a sudden, the cows are fertile, his wife is fertile; everybody in his house is getting blessed and they're prospering. I don't know why you can't relate to that for some reason, but you should. When the blessing's on you, everything around you is supposed to multiply. If you herd cattle, your cattle should multiply! If you herd dollars, your dollars should multiply! When the blessing showed up, that's exactly what happened. Here comes David rejoicing and dancing into the city and God has yet to do anything. All David's operating off of is what he heard, and what he heard was enough. The same God that cursed the Philistines and the Israelites hasn't done a thing. The only thing that's happened is David heard.

A protocol is a rung above a procedure. The major difference between a protocol and a procedure is one of sanctity or intensity. Whereas protocols are to be followed in letter and spirit in all circumstances, procedures can be altered and modified to suit the situation or the requirements. Another difference lies in the fact that policies and procedures are like laws that can be modified to suit present circumstances, whereas protocols are deemed to be the most effective way of doing a particular task. Procedure may not be the best or most effective way, but it tends to be adopted because of its circumstances. Being unskillful with God is the main reason poverty hangs on. Most people think it's sin, but sin isn't the biggest problem facing the church today. Sin was dealt with when Jesus was on the cross. The biggest problem facing the church is how they deal with God. The protocol in their heads have now become procedure. People alter and modify it to suit the situation.

"It fits my circumstance. I have to work on Sunday, so I can't get there." They forget about protocol. When the protocol says "Seek ye first the kingdom of God" (Matthew 6:33), then first becomes first. First is not second. First doesn't come down the pipe when I feel like it. First doesn't come into the situation when I want it to. First doesn't come alone when I think it just happens to fit. First is first! Protocol says to put God first, trust Him first, and do it the way He wants it! There's a difference between procedures and protocols because when God says, "This is the way I want it done," once you know better, you do better. It doesn't become about you in terms of what you think, what you want, how you see it, and your opinion.

A group of Christians were asked what changed their view in terms of homosexuality. "Tell us specifically what you read in the Bible that caused you to change your mind." They had no answer for that, only "Society has changed." Put your hands on the ark; dead. Look in it like you shouldn't have; dead. Why didn't it happen to the Philistines? Because they're not children of covenant. Therefore, they can handle it any way they want to. It doest't matter because all they're going to get from it is a curse. When the ark gets into the hands of those who believe and those who know better, when it ended up at Obededom's house (a righteous man who revered and respected God and who was an honorable man towards God) now what was curse to those who thought they could deal with it any way they wanted is a blessing to him, and all his stuff is looking good. All of his clothes are coming together. All of his Camelacs are stacking up in the driveway. Everything's starting to happen. He's getting blessed to the point where the king said, "I want to come and see what's going on in this man's house." Obededom said, "If you don't want it, can I have it?" The blessing is on your life, and if you don't want it, can I have it? I'll take it!

The same blessing, as it moved through time, cursed one and blessed another. It isn't God who arbitrarily shows divine chastisement or divine benediction, but rather it's a response to how we deal with Him. We think if we're being corrected it's divine chastisement and if we're being blessed, it's divine benediction. However, only God who decides how it comes, and He does it in such a way that makes us feel like it's unfair because we're doing the best we can. So many people get lost in the place of chastisement because they think they've been doing what they need to do, but wonder why it isn't working. Are you following procedure?

Oftentimes retribution is the restorer of reverence. You want to see somebody get real reverent for God? Let them hit rock bottom. All of a sudden they're in the church more than the chairs are. It's retribution that often revives reverence. It's during troubled times that we tend to

97

find the most clarity. Why do we have to experience calamity to get the most clear? We seem to get more clarity as our situation gets worse. You get focused when your butt is getting handed to you. All of a sudden you need God, you're in the church and singing and praising. Then when things start going well, you stop showing up to church, you're mad, you unfriend the church, you act all kinds of fool because you don't need God anymore. You have no understanding of protocol. Protocol would tell me that I need God in the good times and the bad times. I need God, period, because He's God and I'm not. When I bring my supply, I can't take it back because God is always, always expecting me to follow protocol.

People know who God is in your life by how you handle Him. You don't treat your wife like a side chick or else you'll get a side chick. The Bible says if you receive a man as a righteous man, you get a righteous man's reward. If you receive your wife as a wife, you get the wife's reward. If you receive your husband as a husband, not just a honey-do, not just a paycheck, you get the husband's reward. When you receive your brothers and sisters as your brothers and sisters in Christ, you get that reward. When you receive your pastor as your pastor, you get that reward. But it's funny how people don't think of protocol when it comes to how you deal with the church. I've watched people serve and then just walk away and leave you completely hanging. No notice, no nothing. It doesn't matter to them. How can you deal with the institution of God that way? You've lost protocol.

It's one thing to teach about the blessing being on your life, but it's another to show you that if you're unskillful with the things of God, that which was meant to bless you will hurt you. Their response from God was not initiated by God. In any of those circumstances, God did not initiate them, He merely responded. He said if you're going to treat Me like I'm just a box that you can peek into; dead. If you think that as I'm riding on this cart that I shouldn't have been on in the first place, that I'm supposed to be carried by hand, by the Levitical priesthood, and you thought it was good enough to throw Me on a cart and carry

Me into town, you don't know how to deal with the blessing! You don't know how to deal with My presence! Then you think that I needed your help and you put your hand out to help Me? Child, bye! I'm God all by Myself; I didn't need your hand, you need Mine.

Uzzah was just trying to help, but he brought his help in the wrong way. If he wanted to help, he should have fallen back and said, "King David, didn't God tell us to do this a certain way?" That would have helped. You want to help? Fall back and pray for David. God, please reveal to him this is not the way to do this. Uzzah would still be around if he'd have handled it right.

It's one thing to teach and preach on the idea that you're blessed and the blessing is on your life. We know that Jesus died so that the blessing of Abraham can come on your life, but what good does it do us if we don't know how to interact with it? It's funny how people are believing for their healing, but they stay home from church. They think they're too sick to come to church and they've gotten into procedure and out of protocol.

Even if you have to wheel me in on a stretcher, the place where I want to be is in the presence of God. When I'm in the presence of God, miracles happen, victory comes, my overcoming happens! When I'm in the presence of God, my answers come and my healing comes! I don't want to be anywhere else but in the house because when I'm in the house, I understand protocol. You may get people whispering in your ear, "Um, you're probably too sick to go to church today." Are you crazy? The devil is a liar! Uzzah, quit playing with me!

When God says, "Seek me first" it means first. It means in all that I do, He's first. In all that I am, He's first. In all that I own, He's first. That's when you understand that God wants to be the God of Abraham, Isaac, and Jacob. God wants to be your God and He wants you to be His people. He doesn't want anything to come between you and Him. He wants to be first! That way when you acknowledge Him, when you want to see people who are walking in victory, it's despite their circumstances.

You have no idea what I had to fight to get here today! You have no idea what I had to fight to come up and serve God. You have no idea what I had to fight to answer the call! But it's those people who said, "I'm putting You first, despite my circumstances, I'm putting You first despite this situation," who see the hand of God. They're the ones who are blessed beyond measure. They're the ones God is leading and blessing their children, their children's children, their houses, their cars, their stuff! God is moving to enhance the whole household. They made the decision "for me and my house—You can take my life."

Some of you, you can't even get there. You don't understand it. That's because you haven't been through anything. I'm talking to the people who have had to fight stuff that they couldn't tell you if they wanted to. If they told you the truth about what they were doing last night or the attack they had to go through to get here this morning, you would be afraid. You would cringe. I'm talking to those people because they understand that "if you don't want it, can I have it?" It's there for you whether you want it or not! And you can keep letting it be a curse to you through your stubbornness, but "as for me and my house, we will serve the LORD!" (Joshua 24:15).

The thing that cursed the Philistines was the same thing that blessed Obededom and all of his house. The same presence of God, the same manifestation of the blessing. The difference between them and me? I know how to deal with it. Keep Him first. In everything, acknowledge Him that He will direct my path for His ways are higher than my ways. And when I deal with Him, we're not equals. I get down low and prostrate myself. I don't have to be told that I'm nothing; I know that I'm nothing, but He is everything!

I heard someone say one time, "Get it together or forget it forever." Isn't that something? I don't know about you, but I'm going to get it together. I can't forget it. Oftentimes we find ourselves in places where we make decisions that are not based on what God said or wanted. We make them based on what we wanted; we made them based on our lack of faith. It's a lack of faith not to do what God told you to do as He told you to do it. It's a lack of faith to say you have to go to work instead of church. What you are saying to God is that He is not the provider and your job is. When you say you're not going to tithe because you don't have money, what you're saying is that your rent and your electric are your god. He didn't say just *do* it, He said do it *first*.

Sometimes you think it's just about money, but it's not. It's about your heart towards Him. It's not procedure, it's protocol. He wants to know when He walks in the room if your knee will buckle to Him, or will it buckle to APS? Will it buckle to SRP? He wants to know who He is to you. When we read in Ephesians 3:20 that God deals with us according to the power that worketh in us, now we begin to see some things. God dealt with the Philistines according to what worked in them. God dealt with Obededom in accordance with how He worked in him. God dealt with David in accordance to the measure of what was working in him.

If you're walking in a curse, in problem after problem, and the blessing doesn't seem to be working in your life, if you don't want it, can I have it? I'll take it! I like when He blesses my socks off. I don't need socks on anyway. I love it! That doesn't mean I won't walk into calamity; I've had calamity. The Bible says many are the afflictions of the righteous (see Psalms 34:19). That means I'm going to walk into many problems, but the difference between me and someone else is my God! He's well able to do exceedingly, abundantly more than I can ask or think. I got answers! When the problem shows up, God shows up. When the enemy comes in like a flood, He says He'll raise up the standard! (see Isaiah 59:19) That means I have help!

Like I said, if you don't want it, can I have it? It's not helping you, so I'll take it! But if you want it, you'd better learn how to do things the right way. I've watched people come to church and say, "God, bring me a boyfriend/girlfriend, a spouse, or a job." Then when He brings them a job or a spouse, that job, that husband/wife, that thing they asked for takes them right out of the church. All the while as they're going out the door, they're talking about how God has blessed them. They're so blessed, they're walking straight off the cliff to hell. Next thing you know, they're sitting at home with no job, and no spouse.

Now Satan wears on them. "See? You shouldn't have done that. See how you messed up?" Here we are praying you back into the church, "God, we just pray right now, we come against all principalities and powers and spiritual wickedness that they would just come back unto our church. We'll love them!" All the while Satan is working on them saying, "Don't go back there. They don't like you. If they liked you, they'd chase you. They'd find out what's going on with you. You just need to stay home. I love you. It'll just be me and you; no mamas, no cousins… and every chance I get, I'm going to hit you with a shoe."

And then there's that moment when you've been praying it through and finally the thought hits your head, "I have to go back home so I can learn that the next time this stuff comes into my life, I'll know how to deal with it. Not according to procedure, but according to God's protocol."

I know to keep Him first in everything; to keep Him first in my job, my finances, my relationships, and in my life. God doesn't want part of you, he wants ALL of you! Every little piece of you, God wants. But it's not without benefits.

My dad would tell me, "Get you one of them good government jobs because they have the best benefits." I've got me a good kingdom job, which has the best benefits; better than Obama care, better than your mama's care. God said "Cursed is everyone that hangeth on a tree" and "Jesus died that we would be redeemed from the curse of the law so that the blessing that was Abraham would come onto you." The ark was a representation of the presence of God and the ark was used to teach them how to reverence His presence. The challenge is He now lives in a temple that was not made with hands. His presence is on the inside of you, which means now you don't need an ark to show up to reverence His presence because His presence goes where you go. Now that makes perfect sense when He told Joshua that "everywhere you put your foot, I have given you." He was letting him know, "I'm going with you. So when you go into battle, I am with you. When you run to that giant, I am with you. When you run into that situation, I am with you." Now, He resides in you.

How can you not know the blessing is with you? You're waiting for something to happen; it already happened. You're waiting for something to go down; it already went down. You're waiting for a sign; He already gave it. You're waiting for something miraculous; the supernatural has already occurred. You're waiting for the spectacular. If you don't want it, can I have it? I don't know about you, but I want it all. If you don't want a piece of this cake, I want some of the piece you have. I'm not greedy because I'll share it with you, but I want a little bit more than what I've got.

I remember times when things would go wrong in my company and I would beg to say I couldn't go to service that night. If I didn't fix that problem by the next day, it was going to cost thousands of dollars, but five o'clock was quitting time. I knew that problem would be there the next day, so I made my decision: I'm going to church. Some of you don't have the faith for that, but that's okay because we're going to get you there. David was out there dancing his heart out because he heard. He danced so bad he made his first wife upset.

He said, "I haven't even begun." It was all based on what he heard. His faith set in, and when faith set in, he realized that if God blessed Obededom, He'd bless him. All God had to do was get him back where he belongs and deal with him correctly. With every seven steps they sacrificed an animal. Do you know how long that would have taken them? It wasn't about the procedure, it was about the protocol. God said, "This is the way you move My presence. If it takes you seven years to get there, I don't care as long as I'm first."

Everything that's fast isn't always right, and the truth of the matter is everything you get fast, you don't treat right anyway. Often, that plate of correction is the platform for your understanding. You don't tend to understand God until you get in a situation where you need Him.

The reason David responded by faith was because he heard. If you're struggling, find somebody else who isn't and start rejoicing by faith. There are plenty of people who you can walk up to and say, "Just tell me about the blessing on your life." I'm not talking about crazy stuff, I'm talking about the real deal. I'm talking about people who are just blessed and God is moving in their life. Get with them and ask about their new house, and as they start telling you, you just start gettin' it, knowing that you're next, that your miracle's on its way. When you learn how to rejoice with others, God will move because that's protocol! You may not see your physical healing in your body, you may not feel it, you may not experience it. However, you're going to have to do like David did and dance with all your heart, knowing it's about to happen, that it's done, and the blessing is on your life. You may not feel it, you may not see it, you may not have heard it, but when you move by faith, that's protocol.

I challenge you to want it and to walk in it. But, if you don't want it, can I have it? I love the blessing like a fat kid loves cake. I want to walk in it all the days of my life, and all I care about is if I'm pleasing to God. I want to do everything according to protocol, because as long as I'm doing it according to protocol, He's got me and the blessing will manifest. People say, "Oh, that's a blessing. That's a nice car! God just blessed you!" No, I'm blessed. My blessing produced that. My blessing will produce my next house. My blessing will produce the money I need for my kids to go to school. My blessing will produce the things that I need. It's not the blessing of the stuff, it's the blessing that's on my life. It's the presence of God functioning and operating. Not only am I going to be blessed, everything concerning me is blessed.

Yesterday, we were pulling out of our garage and somebody had weeded and cut our lawn. We know who it is. One time, we were coming home from Wednesday night service. We have a neighbor who's touched in terms of strung out. I see him walking on the side of the road and he rushes my car like he's going to do something. I have to admit to you that I had a moment where I lost the vocation by which I was called. I threw the car into park, swung open the door, and when he saw the light come on and knew who it was, he took off. (Did I tell you that I'm not perfect? My wife was behind me and I didn't know what he was going to do, so a real man's got to do what he's got to do. We can pray it away, too, but I can pummel it away.)

Did I tell you that God'll use your enemies? That happened about three months ago, and he's been out there mowing my lawn ever since. He doesn't even know why, he's just happy to do it. My God is well able to do exceedingly, abundantly more than I could ask or think! I'm so blessed the devil is cutting my lawn! We're working on moving and I'm thinking to myself, "I'm going to have to let God know and tell him where we're going so he can come cut that lawn too."

You're blessed now! That whole grace message has flipped us into a place of thinking God has no expectations of us and that we can relegate protocol down to procedure and then switch it all around. How you do things is way more important, and God wants you to know why and how so that when you put Him first, He is able to move. He can't move in what you won't put Him first. If your finances are struggling, you've to ask yourself if God is first. I guarantee you if you're willing to be honest, He's not first. He might be included, but He's not first. If your relationship with another person is all kinds of catawampus, you need to ask yourself if God is really first in both of your lives, not just yours. When you look to the left and to the right, is God first in their life as well? If your health is all catawampus, you have to ask if God is first.

Here's how you know He's first in your healing. When you're sick, what's the first thing you do? Who's the first physician you call? Is it God, or is it your family doctor? I have nothing against doctors, but the first call I make is to my Healer, then I'll go see the doctor. He'll deal with me naturally while I deal with this thing spiritually, and somewhere between the two we're going to meet in the middle. God wants to be first and when you get protocol straight, once you really settle it in your mind that God's first, you'll see His hand. All of a sudden, everything will become reproductive. You'd better get your dogs neutered and spayed because they're going to start producing like crazy! And it's really going to blow your mind after you get them neutered and spayed and they're still reaping a harvest! Then you're really going to know God is moving! When your bank account starts multiplying, when everything you touch starts to prosper, you'll know. You can look at your spouse and say, "Protocol, baby! We're in it now!"

It's very simple, but you need to do it His way. You can't be "sometimey." You can't be, "Well, I'm in trouble now. I need God so I'm coming to church because I'm in trouble." When you're not in trouble, you still need to be devoted to Him. That's protocol. That's when you recognize the King and recognize He's greater than you. You can't put yourself down when you're low, then all of a sudden when you're big and bad, act like you don't need Him. You missed protocol, because God is still God. It's so important that you learn protocol and you learn how to do things.

My first job was at McDonalds when I was 14 years old, and when I left I didn't leave in a very ethical way. I was working fries and I hated working fries. Back then, I think they made stuff with beef fat so you just smelled terrible. You'd get all that grease on you. I called my parents and said, "Come get me." When I saw them pull out up front, I grabbed the fryers with the fries in them, threw them on the ground, and walked out. I said "You can take this job and—" Don't follow my mistakes, follow my faith. But every job I've left since, I can call up and go back to because I left well. Many people don't know how to leave well. When they need the job, they're the greatest boss in the world. When they don't need it anymore, they leave with no notice, no two weeks, and they don't find their replacement. How you deal with things is a measure of you. Your integrity is shown only when nobody's looking; otherwise it's a performance. Otherwise, it's procedure and not protocol.

Protocol exists, no matter what for me. If you're an honorable person, you're honorable. How you do things matters. How you treat your brothers and sisters matter. You can't walk in anger and disgust towards your fellow brothers and sisters in your church and think you're going to prosper. What are you, stupid? The first thing God says is to love, and the way He knows you're His is by your love for your brethren. You might tithe, but your attitude stinks! Keep your money until you can love. Don't waste your money tithing and hating on people. You'd better get it together or forget it forever. This is protocol. This supersedes all the stuff.

You can give until you have emptied all your coffers; you can put as many golden mice and hemorrhoids in a box as you want, but it doesn't matter. That wasn't what it was about. It was about God blessing those who know His protocol. He'll bless those who know how to deal with Him. When they know how to deal with Him, that means they understand who He really is. How you deal with God tells Him what you see in Him.

If you walk up to me and say, "Hi Gene, how are you doing?" I can tell what you see in me. I'm not mad at you, I can just tell. But I can tell you this much, you have enough sense that when you're in a calamity, all of a sudden I become Pastor Gene. I've seen many a person have no respect for me until all hell breaks loose. I'm like, "I don't even know you. I haven't seen you at church for six weeks!" You know what we do though, and you know why? I need my blessing.

Going Along to Get Along

Genesis 13:1-2 (KJV)

"And Abram went up out of Egypt, he, and his wife, and all that he had, and Lot with him, into the south. And Abram was very rich in cattle, in silver, and in gold."

Prosperity as a whole does not only mean finances, but many people believe that it does not include finances. Total prosperity means health, healing in your physical body, healthy relationships, and joy unspeakable. There's just so much that's included in our prosperity, but I want you to understand that finances are a part of that. It's not all of it, but it's a part of it. So when it says that blessing on Abraham might come upon the Gentiles, then when we read that Abraham was *very* rich, he did not just have a little bit. *Very* rich is more than just rich. The blessing of Abraham now comes upon us through Jesus Christ and Abraham was *very* rich in cattle, silver and gold.

Genesis 13:3-9

"And he went on his journeys from the south even to Bethel, unto the place where his tent had been at the beginning, between Bethel and Hai; Unto the place of the altar, which he had made there at the first: and there Abram called on the name of the LORD. And Lot also, which went with Abram, had flocks, and herds, and tents. And the land was not able to bear them, that they might dwell together; for their substance was great, so that they could not dwell together. And there was a strife between the herdsmen of Abram's cattle and the herdsmen of Lot's cattle: and the Canaanite and the Perizzite dwelt then in the land. And Abram said unto Lot, Let there be no

strife, I pray thee, between me and thee, and between my herdsmen and thy herdsmen; for we are brethren. Is not the whole land before thee? Separate thyself, I pray thee, from me: if thou wilt take the left hand, then I will go to the right; or if thou depart to the right hand, then I will go to the left."

It is interesting to me because I have said this several times, and I think sometimes people think there's a level of arrogance behind when I say this particular statement, but I really want you to understand that there is no level of arrogance. My dad used to say, "I'm not conceited, I'm confident." There's a difference between being conceited in yourself and confident in your God. As I said earlier, some of you need to realize that the job you work at, the only reason that place is still going is because you're there. I know that's kind of hard sometimes to fathom, but if you're blessed to be a blessing, then when they bless you by giving you a job, you are blessing them by keeping their doors open. This is not arrogance; it's an understanding of relationship.

In this passage, God told Abram to leave his family—take your wife and your stuff and go. Lot went with him. Lot wasn't supposed to be there in the first place, but because of the blessing that was on Abraham, they both increased to the point where they couldn't live together. The blessing was on Abraham, it wasn't on Lot, but Lot's proximity to Abraham, his association, his environment, and his influence was so great that it started to rub off on Lot.

Now when I show up to anything that I'm involved in, I am confident (not conceited) that the blessing that is on me will make room for me. Have you heard the statement, "Go along to get along"? It invokes a couple of things. The first challenge it invokes is the idea that if I'm going to go along to get along, oftentimes I may be put into a situation where I'm forced to deal with something illegal, immoral, or unethical.

I remember what was probably one of the lowest points of my life. I was arrested for stealing a Christmas tree (which I didn't steal). I had a friend who always would say he would do something. He was one of those talkers. He said, "I want to cut down a Christmas tree, and I'm going to cut it right off of somebody's front lawn." I said, "Whatever." So I pulled up next to one and said, "There it is!" Lo and behold, he did it.

I learned two things from that situation. I'd done my share of stuff that was far worse than Christmas tree–oriented things and had never been in trouble with the law, and here I was in trouble with the law over a stupid Christmas tree. That was the most expensive Christmas tree ever. I had to pay those people for the tree and it cost me a lot of money but it disappeared, and never became an issue. Long story short, I went along because I just wanted to see if he'd really do it. I ended up going along to get along and it put me in the wrong situation.

Oftentimes when you hear, "Go along to get along," you think, "Is this going to put me in a place where I do not want to be?" It could possibly mean that I have to trump myself; I have to overcome my better judgement. I have to subdue what I believe in (my morality, my feelings, and my understanding) in order to go along with something I may not agree with.

The second issue of "go along to get along" would cause some people to think, "Well, I've got to give up my idea. If I just go along to get along, then what I want never comes to pass and I'm always finding myself as a doormat for other people."

Oftentimes, we think as a Christian that it means we have to be a doormat for others. You find this more evident in church. Some people come to church just to prey on other people. They come looking for something—money, a ride, stuff, and it's always a problem. There is never a place of their own dependency on God; it's always, "Can you help me? Can you do something for me?" They come strictly for the purposes of molesting the church. They're not coming to say, "Can I bring something? If you're coming to pick me up, how about I treat you to some Starbucks? How about I do something for you?" It's never that. What they tend to do is manipulate you into a place to make you think that it's your Christian obligation.

In the story of Phillip, he was translated to speak to the eunuch (see Acts 8:26-40). He literally passed a whole bunch of people who could have heard the gospel, but he was on divine appointment and he passed this whole gang of folks to speak to one person. Every single person is not my ministry. While people want you to think that's what it is, that's not the case. Just because you have a need does not mean that I'm the one to fill it. Unless God speaks to me and moves me in that direction, any seed I've sown into you will not produce. I'm to be directed and led by God in the things that I do. So if I now have to feel obligated, if I have to feel a certain way about it, then something's wrong. Whatever I do, I should do out of the conviction and the faith in my heart, not the nature of your sob story.

When we hear "go along to get along," it almost implies that I now have to crush my will in order to get along with you. I now have to press down what it is I want and I desire. I have to give up my hope, my dream, in order to go along. This can conjure up many different things in people. If I have my own ideas, hopes, and dreams, I don't understand why I have to give them up to be associated with you. I don't understand that. This lies in the concept of unity. Here, Abraham is saying to Lot, "Look, your people are fighting with my people. I need this to stop because I understand the power of unity. If we're going to be unified, I can separate from you and have unity." That's an interesting concept. Most of us, in order to find unity, we feel we have to "go along to get along" so that we can have togetherness and have unity. Abraham said, "I need you to leave so I can have unity." Sometimes, the things you are unified about, you won't find anybody, so if they can leave you, let them.

I can't leave what I'm unified to. Unity takes on a certain understanding. I could be unified with you, meaning I have similar understanding and similar interests. We're now "like-minded." Paul said, "I have nobody likeminded like Timothy who I can send unto you" (see Philippians 2:20). In other words, Paul said, "I need you to be taken care of as a church, but I don't have anybody who thinks like me except Timothy, so I'm sending him to you. When he arrives, I'm going to be happy he showed up." He didn't say, "I need to hear the report back of what he did." I already know what he's going to do because he thinks like me; he's like-minded.

If you're like-minded, you don't have to fight to be like me. If you're on my staff and you're like-minded, you will treat people like I would treat people and you don't have to work hard at it. You don't have to be like, "Oh my God, I can't stand people! Child, these people get on my nerves!" You don't have to work and overcome the fundamental differences. There is no substratum of envy and strife that would cause you to come against the plan as soon as I leave your sight. If you're like-minded, then the similarities between us become the very bond which holds us. Therefore, when we are separate from each other, you are like me even though you are not near me, and that brings unity.

Now here's the problem: what if I'm different from you? People believe that if I'm different from you, I cannot exist with you. But how do we explain that in regards to music? Music is harmony, and I can have unity with music and not be the same instrument as you. So now in my unity, I have to find a way to bring all of me to integrate with all of you. Now it's not just about are we exact or identical; it's that we are different, yet complimentary. We are synergistic and syncopated in the way we function so that when we move, we move like music. When we move, we are in harmony together. What you don't have, I have. What you have, I can do and help you when you can't because we have come together in a way that we have taken the best of me and mixed it with the best of you and now we have unity.

The last one is the unity of submission; the unity of meekness. It's when I come into a situation and say because of what's going on, I submit myself. It is the understanding of capitulation. I say, "You know what? I might be able to do this better than you, or I might not. But I'm here to see the purpose done. So if you need me to sweep the floor, I'll sweep the floor. Whatever it is you need me to do, I will capitulate under the understanding of submission and meekness and say that while I believe I might be able to make a greater contribution, I will bring whatever contribution is necessary for the greater common good so that God can be glorified in all of us." Or I can be one of those individuals that until you recognize my gift, I won't do anything. Until you understand that I'm a preacher, if you don't let me preach, I will not submit. This is the very nature of Jezebel. The truth of the matter is if you won't sweep a floor in the church, you will not preach, ever. If there are some aspirations in your head and you won't serve... do the coat.

We were at our staff retreat and one of the senior staff members said that one of the things that shocked him when he first came to our church was that I was cleaning the toilet in the bathroom. You just don't find pastors doing that. Well, when you're the chief cook and bottle washer. you do what you gotta. But I want you to understand something. If I have to do it, so do you.

I know that the premise of your thinking is that you get a leg up and you don't have to go through what I went through. Somehow because I've somewhat arrived in some people's heads, I'm supposed to reach back and allow you to step over the things I had to do so that you don't have to do them.

While that certainly could work for your children, I do say that would build a problem with your kids that would cause them to never value what they have. This is why we have trust fund babies who do not value or appreciate what they have been given because it has never been earned. Everybody's going to have to earn just like I did because there's a cost. It's like in the immortal words of one of the greatest philosophers ever, BB King, "I'm payin' the cost to be the boss, baby." My mom used to tell me that in our house. What does that mean? "I pay the mortgage." Now, all of a sudden, unity is forced because your existence is no longer a privilege.

Unity can come through submission which can be voluntary or involuntary. But the truth of the matter is that true unity can never come through involuntary submission. I can force you to do something, but that doesn't mean you agree. There are times when people will do things and don't agree, and now I don't have the benefit of synergy.

How many times have you found that a husband and/or a wife will capitulate to each other out of compromise which many people think is a good thing. However, compromise to me is a terrible thing. Compromise means that somebody wins and somebody loses. Think about it this way: If I wanted to open the window and you say, "No, I don't want to open the window, I'll turn on a fan," that might come as a compromise, but if I wanted fresh air, then I lost. The nature of my request would then be indicative of what I'm trying to accomplish. If I do not understand the end run, I can put myself at a place where I compromise without a win-win.

God never asked you to compromise. The world has twisted us into believing that compromise works. So when God's Word says one thing and the world wants us to compromise and do something else, we begin to take that which is finite and make it abstract. In order to make it abstract, at that point it is subject to interpretation. Now because it's subject to interpretation, I have lost the very nature of what it was and blurred the line so greatly to the point where now compromise has occurred.

I don't believe in compromise; I believe in win-win. "Win-win" means I seek to understand before I'm understood. Before I can deal with you I need to understand you. Then I know that what you're asking for is fresh air, so now the resolve is that I put on a jacket and open a window. Now you have what you want and I have what I want and we have win-win, not compromise.

The challenge becomes with having unity through submission. How many times as husbands and wives have you gone along with something that you did not agree with and you called it submission? But what happens is after it didn't work, you're the first one in line to say, "I told you so!" This is why your spouse never wants to involve you in anything. You wonder why they don't tell you anything and it's because last time they needed your support, not just your acquiescence. They didn't need your false harmony; they needed you to get behind it to make it work. And the reason it didn't work was because you were not together in unity.

The Bible says. "How can two walk together unless they agree?" (See Amos 3:3.) What that person needed from you is not for you just to acquiesce, but they needed you to go along to get along. They need you to get involved and say, "I believe this is going to work and I'm going to bring everything I can to help make it work. And if it fails, it will not be because I withdrew." Just acquiescing is false harmony. I see it all the time in counseling, especially between husband and wife. One wants to be there and one doesn't. It's always easy to know which one doesn't and that's the one I start in on first. The truth of the matter is, if you don't want to be there, neither do I.

The concept of submission leads people to think certain things. "If I have to submit to you, if I give up my rights, you might hurt me. Now I can become your victim." That's what happens with submission. People fear it. Jesus becomes the example pattern of complete power under total control. He said, "Whatever you see Me do, I saw my Father do and I'm submitted to My Father and that's why I do what I do. Everything I did, He did and I watched Him do it. Now because He did it, He led me and that's why I'm doing it and I do nothing of Myself." That's submission.

Now, was He being taken advantage of? No. How do you take advantage of the willing? The only time an advantage can be taken against a person is when they don't want to do something. So then that means that the necessity of my want has to become predicated upon the greater common good. Because if it's not upon the greater common good, then it's upon my personal life and what I want. Now all of a sudden the reason I'm ever taken advantage of in any situation is because I never really became clear on what it is that I want, yet I blame everyone else.

One of the things we tend to do is protect people from themselves. By that, I mean sometimes there are people who are so zealous but they have no skill. They want to serve, serve, serve. "I just want to serve God! I love God! I want to serve!" And then they burn out, and the first thing they do when they burn out is to turn around and blame the church. "Ya'll use me too much."

Hold on. First of all, if you were serving us you weren't serving the right person. If you're trying to get close to me, you missed it. You ought to be trying to get close to God because I can't help you. When you get into a situation, I can't heal your physical body. I can't increase your bank account. Maybe some, but not a lot like God can. So you need to understand that your connection is based on the undergirding of what you want and the clarity behind what you want. If you want to serve God, then you serve Him.

But sometimes people don't have the filter to keep themselves at the appropriate place and to pace themselves. So when they burn out like a top, they're mad at the church because the church utilized their services beyond the specifications in which they were comfortable. Because they did not know how to self-govern, they're now mad at the organization and not at themselves. The truth of the matter is, I don't keep count of how I serve God. When I get that call at 0-dark-thirty, it is what it is. It's what we do. It comes with the job. This is the life I have chosen.

One of my favorite, best all-time movies is "The Godfather." In one conversation they asked, "How come you didn't find out who did it?" He said, "I didn't care who did it. It had nothing to do with business. This is the life we have chosen." This comes with the life. I'm not going to get all twisted and bent out of shape about what comes with the job. This is my job. It's like a doctor saying he doesn't want to see patients. Choose a new occupation! If you're digging ditches and you hate digging ditches, get out and do something else! What you have not brought to the team is unity. You're doing it, but you're not unified. Now if I understand unity, it becomes more about the overall good than it does my own part in it. God is a God of unity. Abraham's like, "Look, Lot, I need you to choose. I don't care which one you choose. You go that way, I'll go this way. But I need you to choose."

You never go to the people in the squabble. He didn't go to the herdsman and say, "You need to leave my herdsmen alone." He went to the one who could make a decision. Sometimes, people want to bait you into things that will disrupt your unity. You have to be careful of people who always want to invite you over to their house, always want to spend time with you privately. Many times what they are doing is implanting their agenda. They're casting vision. One of the surefire signs is when I see people in the church who are always asking, "Why don't you come over to our house? We want to do this with you." When I see that, it's always a red flag. Why doesn't that get done in a more public setting? We're all part of the body.

The spirit of Jezebel never wants to submit to organizational things. We'll have a movie night at the church; they won't show up to that but they'll invite people to their house the next day for a barbecue. They don't want to be seen in an organized fashion because they can't implant their ideas. What they begin to do is to lay an undergirding of decision and strife and it's very subtle. "I don't know why Pastor chose to put Charmin instead of Northern toilet paper in the bathrooms. What do you think about that? I can't believe that so-and-so did such-and-such. I can't believe that First Lady wore that outfit this weekend."

This is the type of stuff that happens. They begin to pick people who are new and young to the body. You can ask every staff member here if I'm telling the truth. It happens all the time. It's a subverted plot in order to disband unity and create strife. Oftentimes you have to be careful going to people in strife because these people only want to pull you into strife and cause you to choose sides. Abraham said, "I'm not choosing sides. You go that way, I'm going this way." If I can't get syncopation, if I can't get harmony, then I need unity. And if I have to get unity at the expense of the relationship, if you can leave, then leave. You would think that Lot would have said, "Hold on. My herdsmen are fighting with who? I'll be right back." I'd go grab all of them and say, "Hey, let's get something clear. If you fight with them again, it's you who's leaving. Pack your stuff."

Abraham understood that peace and unity were more important. Lot was his nephew. Abram was older. By relationship as an elder, Abram should have been able to say, "Knock it off!" Naturally, he had every right to say, "You know what? Go talk to your people. Tell them we ain't going to have this." But he didn't. Spiritually the blessing was on Abraham. Since it was his blessing, he could have easily said, "You need to just go along to get along." He would have been clear and on the right side of God. But he came to Lot and said, "Obviously this has become so great that we cannot exist together."

You have to be careful of things that happen in your life because as you grow in God, some people can't exist with you anymore. You have outgrown them. That creates strife. When you begin to grow faster than someone else, it creates a problem. It's not that I don't like you anymore, I'm just afraid that our relationship has changed. And the fear of our relationship changing can cause me to pull you back in instead of me allowing you to pull me out. Because of that, I now have to find a way to short-circuit what is going on in your life so that when it collapses upon itself, I can be there to pick up the pieces that I've broken and created. Hence, I force unity. At least I think so.

The Bible says that Lot chose for himself. He looked around and saw the best and said, "I'll take that."

Genesis 13:10-13
"And Lot lifted up his eyes, and beheld all the plain of Jordan, that it was well watered everywhere, before the LORD destroyed Sodom and Gomorrah, even as the garden of the LORD, like the land of Egypt, as thou comest unto Zoar. Then Lot chose him all the plain of Jordan; and Lot journeyed east: and they separated themselves the one from the other. Abram dwelled in the land of Canaan, and Lot dwelled in the cities of the plain, and pitched his tent toward Sodom. But the men of Sodom were wicked and sinners before the Lord exceedingly."

Because Lot chose with his eyes, he chose Sodom and Gomorrah. I want you to understand that it is totally normal for a person to want the best, but I don't want the best at the expense of having God's best. When the lust of my eyes comes into play, it's because I believe I don't have. Now I can't be mad at Lot. If Lot knew the blessing was on Abram, he was going to have to choose the best. You can be mad at Lot all you want to, but if I was Lot and I knew the blessing wasn't on me, I'd have to choose the best and hope for the best. The only way that I would prosper is to have luck so I would have to choose the best because that's the only thing I have to hold onto.

Because men are visual people, we tend to be visual about our relationships. We can find ourselves sometimes looking after what we believe to be better. If you're not careful, better will mess you up.

Better often is bitter. The premise, the substratum, the undergirding of success in a relationship as a man is to know that you have the best. When you have the best, you don't want anything from the rest because you recognize that what you have is better. While I may remark about attributes and say, "That's wonderful, that's remarkable, that's noteworthy of this particular individual," nobody has the package like my package, my wife. So thereby because my pack is the package, when I look up at the land and say, "You can go whatever way you want," I am able to forsake what I want first and put myself second because I already have the best.

Now I'm not so enamored about what's coming or what I see out there because I have the best. When your wife or your husband feels like they are the best, they're never threatened by the rest because they know that if you look out upon the land, you'll say, "You know what? I already have the best this world has to offer. So if you want to go this way, I'll go that way." The presence of choice always exposes true motivation. If somebody's in a relationship with you because they don't want to be alone, that's no choice. They didn't choose you, so now when something better comes along, all of a sudden they're just not that into you.

I could stand on the hilltop and say, "This is the best land so I want that. Lot, you go that way." Abraham said, "Because the strife is coming from you, I'm going to let you be first to make a choice." For me to put you first is kingdom. He understood that strife and contention is a problem. For some of you, your home is full of strife. There's always fighting, arguing, and disagreement. There's cussing and all this drama that goes on in your home. Then you leave home and get in your car and you're fighting over what radio station you'll listen to. You get to your where there's more strife. We live our lives in strife, not realizing that blessing and strife cannot exist together.

Abram said, "Listen I need you to resolve this strife. I don't want it done now, I want it done right now." If the contentious people in your life can go, let them because you need to bring your life into a place of peace so that it's not all topsy-turvy. Some people live for drama. They're always saying how much they hate it, yet they create it. They just love it! And if you let them, they'll draw you into it. Now, all of a sudden, you're mad like they're mad. Nobody did anything to you, but you're upset. "The institution and the government and I can't believe they did..." They didn't do anything to you! That was their problem and they brought you into it! Now you're mixed up in the strife and the blessing is like, "I'll wait."

That's why Abram said, "I need God too much. So when you leave, don't look back."

Ephesians 4:1-3
"I therefore, the prisoner of the Lord, beseech you that ye walk worthy of the vocation to which ye are called, With all lowliness and meekness, with long-suffering, forbearing one another in love; Endeavoring to keep the unity of the Spirit in the bond of peace."

It's easy for me to be in unity with people who think like I think. That's wonderful. But what happens when I have to be in harmony with a person who doesn't think the way I think, but I still have to function with them and make music with them? I need to allow their differences to be their differences and allow what I am to augment and offset what it is they do not have, so that although we might be very different, we can still come together and be united together.

What do I do when I need to capitulate myself endeavoring? Did you ever hear anybody say, "That's an endeavor right there"? You know what they're telling you? That's going to be some work. Everything in your life will compete against peace. Everything in the world will try to bring in strife. Paul says to "endeavor." That means to make a painstaking effort to keep that unity and the bond of peace. I'm not going to fight with you in my house. We're going to get along, trust me! Because if we don't get along, you've got to leave. As for me and my house, we're going to serve the Lord! So we have to get along. We have to find a way to dwell together, to come into agreement. I need to find a way to get behind you or you get behind me, one or the other, but somebody must find a way to bring some unity as my blessing depends on it! My life depends on it! My prosperity depends on it! You can't be in my house causing problems! And if you can leave, then leave. I'm going to go along to get along. I'm going to escalate the purpose above my feelings.

This is where pride has to be dealt with. "You mean to tell me that I'm to serve and then one day I'll be in a leadership position?" Yeah, that's how it works. You don't believe me? Sign up for the military and tell them you want to be a general. You ever notice they're all old? I know you don't think they go out recruiting old folks. They were young when they started.

Psalm 133:1-3
"Behold, how good and how pleasant it is for brethren to dwell together in unity! It is like the precious ointment upon the head, that ran down upon the beard, even Aaron's beard; that went down to the skirts of his garments, Like the dew of Hermon, and like the dew that descended upon the mountains of Zion; for there the LORD *commanded the blessing, even life for evermore."*

Now you know I thought they were talking about Zion for a long time. "There" is not Zion; "there" is *unity*. When water hits the top of a mountain and it begins to flow down, it provides for the lush vegetation at the bottom. So the growth of that which is at the bottom is fed by what comes down from the top. When unity is present, when people dwell together, it allows that which is coming down from the Father of lights—every good and perfect gift—to come down unto my life. When there is unity, it is allowed to come down and to produce in the ground of my life. But when strife comes in, it stops that which is coming down and it literally cannot produce in my ground because I am into strife and contention. I don't have time to fight with you! I don't have the patience to fight with you! I don't have the wherewithal to be fighting with you! Notice the psalmist says it's like the ointment that pours down from Aaron's head into his beard. That's a representation of the anointing which starts from the head on down.

You wonder why some of your children act the way they do? It's because you as parents can't get along. It starts from the head and when the head is not right, the children will respond in kind. But when the head gets it together, it falls from the top down to the beard, down to the skirt, and the children start acting right. You're like, "Whoa, what happened?" It had nothing to do with *them* getting corrected, it had to do with *you* getting corrected. Once you come together, you must teach your children how to be in a good relationship and how to provide for their families! It falls from the head on down. When the head's straight, everything else is.

That's why everybody can't be on staff in the church. You have to be in unity. I can't be unified with you in the boardroom, but fighting with you outside of it. I'd rather have somebody with no skill and no talent that can at least be in unity. Unity is everything! I built my home to be in unity. I created space of peace, harmony. We are not identical, but we are syncopated. When my wife moves, I move. When I move, she moves. We finish each other's sentences. We often say the same thing at the same time. Before she met me, she had her own rhythm, her own drums, and so did I. But somehow through time, exposure, and a desire to be together, I learned, "Hey, I might not like this, but I can live with it. I may not agree with that, but I can get over it. I might not want it done this way, but I'm going to back off and let it be." Unity is everything!

The Lord commanded a blessing! That means there is no possibility of disrupting the blessing because God commanded it to come in unity. So if I want to see blessings in my life, I better learn how to go along to get along! It's not about me. It's not about how I feel. It's not about how I think. It's about the greater purpose. I need the blessing to flow!

About two months ago, I received a call from some people involved in this building and they're about as demonic as they come. I hung up the phone, ready to chew steel and spit nails. Everything in me said, "You know what? We're going to settle this old school style." I know you're perfect, but please understand I am a flawed vessel. Something in me said, "Call your daddy." So I called Pastor Ricky and I said, "Hey, here's what happened."

He listened to me and said, "I told you this before and I'm going to tell you one more time. Don't you let people bait you into strife. If you're going to walk in the blessing, everything's got to be about unity and peace. The moment you get into strife, you get out of your blessing." I was like, "Okay, thank you, Sir! You have a wonderful day! Bye!"

He was right. They were engaging me because I had finally gotten clear about how to stay out of that. What you have to know is that Satan will use even people close to you. He'll stir them up and you'll wonder, "Okay, where is this coming from? I thought we were cool. I thought we were good!" But Satan stirred it up to bait you and the moment you go off on them and give them a piece of your mind, you've just stepped outside of your blessing. "I kept it real! You know me, we handle this like some gangsters or we can be some gentlemen!" Are you serious? My blessing depends on how I respond. I don't have the ability to allow you to bait me in! I've got to stay out and let that strife go! "My name is Wes, I am not in that mess. My name is Paul, that's between ya'll."

There are some people in your life, all they want is drama. Let them go! They're toxic; they're trying to keep you from your blessing and if you want to walk in it, unity is the key! If they won't submit and capitulate for the greater good of the family, then guess what? "Well, we are family. We're kinfolk. You can't treat me like this. I gave birth to you!" Yes, and thank you, but that was awhile ago. We were unified then.

The concept of dwelling in unity together and the ability to keep that unity means that peace comes by virtue of the environment which I set. The Bible says you can't have peace *of* God unless you have peace *with* God (see Philippians 4:6-7). Peace is really not the issue, however. I don't have to pray for peace or ask for peace. All I really have to do is create an atmosphere. God commanded the blessing and He's the one who gave me peace. He said, "My peace I leave with you, not peace as the world giveth but I give unto you my peace" (John 14:27). So it is not my desire to have to seek after peace. I have to seek peace with other people. But seeking peace with somebody means to create an environment of peace. You know how many times I've apologized to people for stuff I didn't do just to keep the relationship? I just swallow my pride and say, "You know what? I'm sorry. I didn't mean to force you to do what you did." I don't say it like that, I say it with a little more tact and discretion, but you get my point. I can capitulate for the greater good.

Do you remember where Abram said, "I need you to go whichever way you need to go." There are two issues with that that need to be dealt with. Why did he tell Lot that his enemies were present? That holds the key to all of this. What Abraham was telling him was, "We're in the midst of hostile territory. I can't be fighting with you. I've got to watch out. I'm in hostile territory. My enemies are behind me, they're pressed on the side of me, they're in front of me, and my God has created a buffer around me because I stay in peace." So that means I can be *in* the world and not be *of* the world. But if my enemies are sitting around watching, waiting for an opportunity, I don't have the time, I don't have the focus, I don't have the patience to be dealing with you when I'm in the midst of scarcity, in the midst of an attack, in the midst of problems, and you want me to fight with you, the very person who should be on my side? The very person that should be in this fight with me? I don't have time to argue with you because now you are taking my focus away from my God who is delivering me and delivers!

Some of you don't realize you're in the midst of a fight, a problem, a challenge, and the strife that you constantly allow in is stealing your deliverance, until you say, "I have to get some unity. I have to get some peace. You have to go. I know I'm in love with you, but you have to go. If I don't get you out, I will never make it because I'm pressed on every side. I'm getting attacked from every angle."

There are some people reading this today who know exactly what I'm talking about when the attack is coming from all angles and you're like, "I need some peace! If you're going to be my child, you better act like my child. If you're going to be my wife, you'd better act like my wife. If you're going to be my husband, act like my husband, because we're in this fight together!"

Abraham said, "Lot, I love you. I took you with me. I disobeyed God to have you in my life. I left what God told me to allow you to come into my life, but you have to go. You weren't supposed to be sleeping in my bed with me, but you have to go. God told me not to get yoked up unequally, but I did it anyway, and now you got to go." He said, "I can't fight them and fight you. I can't defend what I have and have to defend it from you as well." Endeavoring takes a painstaking effort. When we get into strife, it causes us to compete for resources. It causes us to compete for focus and attention. Because you have a problem, now I'm worried about your problem when I have problems of my own! My issues have issues! I don't have time to be worried about yours. I don't mind helping you, but help comes in a certain way.

It's funny how people want to counsel with me until I have to tell them what they don't want to hear. You want to know why? I'm not there to hang out with you. I'd rather hang out with my wife. When you come to me for counsel, I'm there to help you. We're there to fix it. If I have to counsel you more than three times on the same issue, that means you're trying to use me as a garbage can because all you want to do is spew out garbage and I'm not interested. If you want to come and change, we'll do that. Sufficient motivation is necessary, and if you have it, we'll do it. But I can't get into strife and contention with people who just want combat.

I've had people say, "Well, I don't know if that's what the scripture means." Go look it up! We're not going to argue about it. Only a fool argues with a fool. You best believe I studied it through over and over and over again before I taught it. I sometimes put in 40–50 hours of study for one message. When I come out here and talk, I'm not talking off the top of my head. I'm trying to get clear because I know that if I'm clear, if I'm a student of the Word, then I can be a minister of the Word. You can't be a minister if you're not a student. That's absolutely important. But do you have any idea how hard that would be if my house was in strife? Trying to study, trying to get clear, trying to pray with strife all around me? No, no. We're going to stay together.

Genesis 13:14-15
"And the LORD said unto Abram, after Lot was separated from him, Lift up now thine eyes, and look from the place where thou art northward, and southward, and eastward, and westward, For all the land which thou seest, to thee will I give it, and to thy seed for ever."

As soon as Lot left, God said to Abram, "I will give you all that you see from every direction." Lot chose *a* direction, God gave *all* directions. That's why Abraham didn't care. The very essence of faith says that I can forego me to prefer you so that you can choose for yourself. The moment you choose for yourself, everything you choose, God's going to give me that and everything around me. If the blessing is on me, then wherever I go, the blessing goes with me. So my goal is not to produce a blessing, my goal is to produce an atmosphere where the blessing can manifest. I'm constantly at a place where I want peace. I want harmony. I want us to go along to get along.

When I find people who are willing to go along to get along, that means they have elevated their purpose to be in sync with mine. Now we can do something. Now the blessing can flow. If I go into a store and there's automatic strife, I'm done. I don't have to spend my money there, I'll find some other place where I can spend my money. I only involve myself with people I have favor with. When I can sense harmony and favor, that's where I go. That's where I spend money. You know, it's funny every time I do that, I walk in blessing.

We were working on a situation in which we were dealing with various people. One lady called us back and said, "God dealt with me." That's music to my ears. Let's get syncopated, baby! What did God say? "He told me to give you a deal." That sounds like my God! What else did He say? I heard Him say, "Free!" I kid you not, people have walked up to me and said, "God told me to give you this hundred." And I'm like, "No, He didn't. He told you to give me a thousand! You negotiated me down to this hundred, I left the hundred stage about ten years ago!" I'm blessed!

Protect your unity at all cost! If there are people who get under your skin, get them out from under your skin! Put some distance on them. "Look, I love you, but we can't be together because I have to protect me." In the place of unity is where the Lord commands a blessing.

Revelation for the Manifestation

Galatians 3:13 has been the foundational scripture of what we've been studying and it is important for us to understand and discern. Verse 13 tells us that Christ has redeemed us from the curse of the law. We recognize that most people who are in Christ don't necessarily struggle with understanding that they've been redeemed. I think that's the battle cry (or the anthem) for all believers. The challenge I think a lot of believers struggle with is verse 14 which says *so that*.

We rally around being redeemed and we understand that we have been set free, loosed from demonic oppression, loosed from the grip of Satan, and loosed out of hell and into heaven. We can conceptualize and understand that, but do we get the fact that we have been loosed for a reason? Verse 14 explains to you the reason why. It's so that the blessing of Abraham might come on the Gentiles through Jesus Christ that we might receive the promise of the spirit through faith. The writer gives us an understanding that there are two things that come out of our redemption. Number one is that the blessing of Abraham will come upon us, and number two is that we might receive the promise through the spirit.

The challenge I have is that oftentimes we look at our prosperity and the things that God is doing in our lives from a natural perspective. But when we look at the madman of Gadara who had supernatural strength, he had supernatural strength because he was empowered by spiritual things. So then we begin to know that all spiritual things can influence or implement things in the natural and that all natural power is spiritual in nature. Oftentimes we don't think of it this way, but if natural power can be spiritual in nature, then why can't prosperity be spiritual in nature?

What the writer explains to us is that the blessing of Abraham comes upon the Gentiles through Jesus Christ that we might receive the promise—the promise that God made to Abraham that said, "I will give you land, I will bless you, I'll make your name great and I will curse those that curse you." Now I don't know about you, but I could stop there. That's the end of it as far as I'm concerned. It doesn't get any better than that! What he's saying is that the blessing God put upon Abraham now comes upon me. I have access to that by Jesus Christ. My faith in Christ gives me access to the promise. The promise is not natural, the promise is spiritual. He says it comes by the spirit through faith. So that tells us flat-out it's a spiritual thing.

If you want to prosper in the things of God and the things in your life, you better handle the spiritual things right. So many people think that it's about sin, that sin is the greatest problem in the church. It is not! To be honest with you, sin is the least of problems in the church because sin has been dealt with. How people deal, handle, and function causes the greatest problem that we have.

Ephesians 3
"For this cause I, Paul, the prisoner of Jesus Christ for you Gentiles–If ye have heard of the dispensation of the grace of God which is given me toward you: How that by revelation he made known unto me the mystery; (as I wrote afore in few words, By which, when ye read, ye may understand my knowledge in the mystery of Christ) Which in other ages was not made known unto the sons of men, as it is now revealed unto his holy apostles and prophets by the Spirit. That the Gentiles should be fellow heirs, and of the same body, and partakers of his promise in Christ by the gospel, of which I was made a minister, according to the gift of the grace of God given unto me by the effectual working of his power. Unto me, who am less than the least of all saints, is this grace

given, that I should preach among the Gentiles the unsearchable riches of Christ, And to make all men see what is the fellowship of the mystery, which from the beginning of the world hath been hidden in God, who created all things by Jesus Christ, To the intent that now, unto the principalities and powers in heavenly places, might be known by the church the manifold wisdom of God, According to the eternal purpose which he purposed in Christ Jesus our Lord, In whom we have boldness and access with confidence by the faith of him. Wherefore, I desire that ye faint not at my tribulations for you, which is your glory. For this cause I bow my knees unto the Father of our Lord Jesus Christ, Of whom the whole family in heaven and earth is named, That he would grant you, according to the riches of his glory, to be strengthened with might by his Spirit in the inner man; That Christ may dwell in your hearts by faith; that ye, being rooted and grounded in love, May be able to comprehend with all saints, what is the breadth, and length, and depth, and height, And to know the love of Christ, which passeth knowledge, that ye might be filled with all the fullness of God. Now unto him who is able to do exceeding abundantly above all that we ask or think, according to the power that worketh in us, Unto him be glory in the church by Christ Jesus throughout all ages, world without end. Amen."

It is interesting that the book of Ephesians is often referred to as the blueprint of maturity. If you spent a good portion of your life studying this book, you will learn how to be a good Christian. It teaches you in three basic themes of sit, walk, stand.

"Sitting" explains to you who you are positionally in Christ. Where you *sit* is everything, because where you sit in Christ determines if your condition will outweigh your position. Most people do not understand that your condition is not the same as your position, and if you try to climb into your condition to resolve it, you will not make it. You are going to have to learn how to respond to the condition from your position.

"Walking" is how you walk out your Christianity; how you *do* God and not just talk about God.

The last thing that is addressed in the book of Ephesians is how to "stand". In other words, once you have understood your position, once you begin to walk out your Christianity, you will come under attack. It is not *if*, it's *when.* When you fall under attack, how do you respond to it? Paul then says when you have done all to stand, then stand some more.

When you understand this progression, then you begin to see how the maturity of the church is supposed to happen. God is creating a situation for your revelation and this situation you're in is important. It's important because there is a mystery. The mystery has not been revealed prior to this time, but now it is.

As the mystery is being revealed, what is that mystery? We are partakers of His promise! When we believe in Jesus, the blessing of Abraham comes upon us that we become joint heirs according to the promise. We are joint heirs by faith and we access it in the realm of the spirit. We become joint partakers in it and it becomes a mystery, or I should say the mystery is that and that's what begins to be revealed.

Now here's the thing: nobody ever finds God. God was never lost. Because He is *omnipresent* (which means he's *everywhere).* He is not the one who is lost. It is, in fact, you who are lost and now have been found. Whatever we call a mystery is something that has exceeded and goes beyond our intellect. If you don't have knowledge of it, it's a mystery.

I don't know about you, but I like a good whodunit story. But the truth of a whodunit is once you found out whodunit, you're done with it. What begins to happen is, a tension is created between you and the story, not knowing who and the person who wrote it. They know who, but they reveal it to you slowly until you get to the end to see if you were right. It almost becomes, by nature, a created tension allowing you to become so engrossed that it becomes a page turner. You stick through it through the commercials because you have to see who did it because who did it is beyond your intellect. It's something you do not know.

While I may love you, I may know you, I may sit next to you every service in church, I may *not* be clear on everything about you (and it will not come to me just because I sit next to you). You have to reveal some things to me. The very nature of a mystery is the understanding that it isn't something I already know; it's something that I need to know.

When I begin to understand God, I cannot have relationship with Him until He reveals Himself to me. So then the depth of my relationship is not in the depth of my pursuit, it's in the depth of His revealing. That means there could be times when I will chase after Him and He will only reveal what I need to know for that situation. If I follow you somewhere and ask, "Where are we going?" I'm asking you that because I may get tired of following; I may get lost in the following. However, when I know where we're going, I'll meet you there. But God says, "You and I don't have that type of relationship. We have the type of relationship where if you get lost in the following, you are lost. I'm not always going to tell you because I want to know if you will you move when I move. Will you step when I step? Will you believe and follow Me, or are you looking to your own abilities in order to follow?" Revelation then becomes progressive. As I begin to follow, more revelation occurs. So the mysteries of God are never just given; they are revealed, and they're revealed as He wills.

One of the hardest things to do in the midst of circumstances is to keep your expectations high, especially if you've failed many times. When you go through that over and over again, the Bible says hope deferred makes the heart sick. Calamity and trouble in situation after situation begins to redefine our expectation, and because we are creatures of habit, we tend to lower the bar in order to get over it.

When things don't seem to work so well and we've been disappointed so many times, the mindset is formed that "I'm going to lower my expectation in order to defend myself so that as I lower my expectations, when the situation jumps over it I get a win."

Now what begins to occur is that my concept of God, although it's supposed to be universal based on the Bible, it becomes unique to the individual. Now what you're telling me is that who God is to me is different than who God is to you. All of a sudden if I'm the one who was lost and now I'm found, and He searches all of me and knows my heart, then it's not the nature of Him figuring me out that creates my difference. God to you is different than He is to me. God to you might be all-powerful. God to me might be a punisher. It is not God in His revealing Himself to me that creates that, it is me in my search and quest of Him, what I've experienced and my perception of Him.

To prove this point, think about when Jesus asked Peter. "Who do they say that I am?" Then the second question He asked him was, "Who do you say that I am? [Because what they say I am can be very different than what you say I am.]" Notice, Jesus didn't ask Peter "What do I say that I am?" That was never in question. He knew who He was. So Jesus didn't say, "Tell me who I say that I am." He said, "Who do *you* say that I am." This implies that there might be a difference in understanding between who Jesus says He is, who you say He is, and who they say He is. In other words, He said, "Tell Me what they say about Me. Now tell Me what you say."

The truth of the matter is, that which affects you will only be what you say. But here's my problem: Paul says, "For this cause I bow my knee." He said, "I don't want you to be upset about what I'm going through. What I'm going through is for your benefit." He said, "The very nature of what is being revealed to me is coming in what I go through." So that indicates we must have an experience.

When Jesus asked Peter, Peter said, "Thou art the Christ, the son of the living God," and Jesus then said, "You did not figure that out on your own. My Father had to reveal that to you." Because again, God is not found, God is revealed.

So the revelation of who God is requires experience with Him in order to fully discern Him. What is a mystery to you is not a mystery to Him. It's only a mystery is because it exceeds your intellect; that's what makes it mysterious. I cannot stand it when people say, "God works in mysterious ways." I'm like STOP! He's mysterious only to those who don't know Him. Oftentimes the allure of a relationship is rooted in mystery. It's the allure of, "Is he a bad boy, or is he not a bad boy? What's he like? What are his dreams? What are his hopes? What does she like? What does she not like? What's she all about? I wonder what she worries about. I wonder what she fears. I wonder what she loves." It's the mystery of what you don't know. Unfortunately, as relationships progress, if you are not careful the mystery is now gone. Now you know what she doesn't like. You know what foods she likes. You've eaten that food five times in the last six days. What has been mysterious and had such an allure of attraction now has become mundane. When it becomes mundane, we oftentimes stop seeking after the very thing we need.

Experiences are interesting because, believe it or not, your mind will give your experience any definition it can in order for your mind to let it go. Things can happen in your life that you don't understand, and your mind will give you a definition so you can move on. Otherwise, you'll remain hooked. Say you see two people passing each other. One reaches over and touches the other's shoulder, says "Hi," and keeps moving. And you're like, "That was a little bizarre." All of a sudden, in your mind, you've got them sleeping together. You know, it's not (how people say) the "gift of discernment." There's nothing in the Bible that says "gift of discernment"; it's the gift of *discerning of spirits*. What you're operating in is the gift of suspicion. Your suspicion scratches that itch for you and you say, "Oh yeah, that has to be it. That'll work." Whether it's true or not is a whole different ballgame.

Is it possible that our experiences and encounters with God have often been skewed by our own interpretations? If that's the case, then the moment I encounter God, am I ever clear what just happened? When people say, "Man, you were lucky. That was just fortunate!" Do you know what they're saying? They're saying in the moment of a situation, there was no preparation to meet the situation but your supply met you anyway. You might have been unaware of your need and it was met so quickly, or the need being met before the need appeared and the world says that's luck. It's luck only because you have no cognitive understanding of what was about to happen and/or did happen so it was new to you. But to God who knows all things, you need to be careful because what you call luck He calls provision. Because He knew that there was going to be that moment where your need was going to show up, He provided before you even knew the situation!

In the moment where people call it luck, again, luck is the idea that I have a time frame, a dead-end to my encounter. We move away from expecting God to move when we hit deadlines and we move into the idea that we are lucky, or that we need luck, or that I have no luck, or we get into the concept of chance. It's all a matter of time. Anything that is related to gambling is luck and chance. You don't have five days to wait and see which number comes up. You don't have two weeks to figure out whether you've got the right king or ace or spade. You don't have an unlimited measure; it's a finite amount of time that applies pressure to allow you to move out of the situation and into your expectation of luck.

Luck then denotes a certain randomness—whether I'm blessed randomly, was I in the right place at the right time, and did it all happen out of luck or was it God's provision? What moves it away from God's provision is that the clock keeps ticking. So when I find myself in a situation God created for my revelation, because I become geared on the time, I begin to think my God is not going to move. So then I have to find something to do to resolve this problem. I then put it back into the category of luck because anything that's time-sensitive forces a dependence on luck if you're not careful. You are not a child of chance. While your situation may have surprised you, God is not sitting up there saying, "Oh! I didn't see that coming. Jesus, how come You didn't tell me that was about to happen?" You realize that He is not surprised by anything that happens in your life.

You may think that you have been disqualified because of the things you have done. And you have come to the conclusion that God didn't know what you've done, He wasn't there when you did it, and before you did it, He didn't know it was coming. But the truth of the matter is, no matter what you have been through, God saw it coming. He was there when you did it, and He is there afterwards to know if you can get past it yourself. God is not looking backwards; He is looking forward to the next thing He has for you! But if you're not careful, you'll get lost. You'll get stuck and start looking at time and then think you need luck. Then you become a person of limited choices.

The idea of luck implies that when the next card is dealt, I don't know what that card is. That does certainly create a level of mystery, but not all mystery is good mystery (such as when you're waiting for the kindness of strangers, depending upon something to happen, waiting for someone else to do it for you). It's like when people say they have faith. They're like "Oh, I have faith! I've got plenty of faith!" but then they run around the church telling everyone their problems, hoping somebody will help. "Can I get a ride from you? Look, I'm struggling. Can you do this for me?" They beg so much, their hands look like cups. They breed harshness in you. Then you're like, "Well, am I being a good Christian? Am I not being a good Christian?" So you avoid them. You see them coming and you go the other direction. This happens all the time because what people don't understand is that I don't depend upon you. When I'm in the experience, if I allow time to pressure me, then I need you. But if I don't allow the time to pressure me, then I do not need you. What I need is God.

When Paul says in Ephesians 3:20, "Now unto him that is able to do exceedingly, abundantly, above all we ask or think…" then he adds, "according to the power that worketh in us," I have a challenge with that because God is all-powerful all by Himself. He doesn't need me! God said, "I'm God all by Myself!" When Moses asked, "Who do I say sent me?" He said "Tell him I AM sent you." I AM what? "Whatever you want to put behind the I AM, I am." He said, "I am not God because you made Me God, I am not God because you worship Me as God, I am not God because you praise Me as God. I am God because I made Myself God." So then I'm not needed.

But then he tells me it's "according to the power that worketh in me." You mean to tell me that I need God to increase, and what you're telling me is as God increases, so do I? You're almost telling me that *I* have to increase for God to increase. "According to" is a percentage, so I get so many per one hundred. So for every one hundred of God, I need this of you. If I increase the one hundred, I have to increase this to keep the same ratio. So what he is, in fact, telling me is that if I want to see more of God, God has to be large in me for God to be large in what I see. And that means if he says "now unto him who is able to do exceedingly, abundantly above all that you could ask or think *in percent to* the power that works in you," this helps me understand that His increase is tied to my increase. And that means as He increases so do I, and as I increase so does He.

Now, I begin to understand that my situation, my circumstance, the very thing I'm going through, once I realize I need to have that experience with God, then I feel like when I'm wrestling with a problem, when a situation occurs, I often don't like it because it feels uncomfortable. The situation that I'm in, it was indeed my intellect that brought me in, but it is revelation that will have to bring me out.

Einstein said that problems cannot be solved at the level of awareness that created them. This implies that the problem you're in, you created at your level of understanding. In order for you to get out of your problem, you're going to have to go to another level and get a higher-level answer to a bottom-level problem. If your intellect brought you in it, then the only thing that can bring you out is that which is revealed.

The nature of a mystery is the fact that it has yet to be revealed, but the moment it is revealed it is no longer a mystery. So when Paul said that no one knew this up until this moment, but it is now been revealed to us that we are now partakers of the promise, he was saying that it was a secret but it is now no longer a secret anymore. As I am a partaker of the promise, I understand what is now being revealed so the solution to my problem is always in increase to my revelation.

So now I get it! When Jacob was wrestling with God, God touched him in the hallow of his leg and said, "Enough is enough! You simmer down!" But he was wrestling because he had made a decision and said, "I will not stop until you bless me. I will not stop until I get that blessing." That means there has to be a moment, an intersection of my need, and a problem by which I begin to wrestle with God. But God wants to know, Are you going to give up? Are you going to back off, or are you going to say that this experience you're in is necessary?

What you have done is, you have created a situation for your revelation because revelation can only be applied where a need is met. You have never had a revelation that didn't meet your need. Otherwise, what is the purpose of revelation? Revelation is never encountered until there is a situation. The point of my encounter is always the intersection of my situation, my circumstance, and the revelation. Not always the provision, because remember I'm supposed to believe that I'll receive and then I'll have what I need. So if I wait for the provision to occur, then it's likely I'll run out of time. But if I can get the revelation, then time no longer becomes valid because once I have the revelation, manifestation follows revelation.

So many people are waiting for the manifestation and they don't have the revelation. If I am to walk in what is revealed, then once it's revealed I have it. It's just a matter of doing it. But because people are so carnally tied to seeing the manifestation of something, they don't realize that the most important thing is to solve the mystery. Every situation in your life creates mystery. Will God answer my _____? Will He solve _____? Will He give me _____? Will He take care of _____?

Nobody worries about what's been revealed. If you truly know that God is your supply, what would you ever worry about? If you truly know that you have relationship with Him, what would you worry about? You wrestled with Him and won, and He got to the point where He said, "Look, I'm going to give you a limp to slow you down because I'm done. Here's your blessing, you can have it." New revelations always require new levels and the only way to grow to a new level is to be stretched beyond your own abilities. If I want you to come to a different level, I have to get you beyond who you are.

The very nature of your growth indicates the growth in God. If He begins large in me, He becomes large in what I see, then He's going to have to create a situation for my revelation.

Hebrews 12:14-16 (MSG)
"Work at getting along with each other and with God. Otherwise you'll never get so much as a glimpse of God. Make sure no one gets left out of God's generosity. Keep a sharp eye out for weeds of bitter discontent. A thistle or two gone to seed can ruin a whole garden in no time. Watch out for the Esau syndrome: trading away God's lifelong gift in order to satisfy a short-term appetite."

God said, "Jacob whom I loved and Esau who I hated." I had to think about this whole exchange between Jacob and Esau. The name Jacob means "leg-puller." When Esau was born, Jacob was holding his leg trying to pull him back in so he could come out first. He wanted to get the blessing! When you hear somebody say, "You're pulling my leg," that's where that comes from. "Jacob" also means *trickster*.

I had always thought that Jacob tricked Esau, and if that's the case, the challenge I have is why is God so mad with Esau? I began to think about that. Esau was in a situation where he was hungry, and he was dumb enough to trade God's blessing for some food.

It was not an indication of Jacob's desire to have the blessing that became the problem, it was Esau's lack of regard for it. You can want something all you want, but God wants you to desire Him, He wants you to go after Him. The one He can't stand is the one the blessing does not matter to. Here, what Esau has done is he has shortchanged a lifelong blessing that would have produced what he needed in time. But because he had no regard for the blessing, he decided, "I'm going to make a permanent decision in a temporary situation." That's why the adage says to watch out for the Esau syndrome.

I hate commercials and TV has become a bunch of commercials. On TV, sometimes you hear "Beeeeeeep! This is a test of the emergency broadcasting system." It's a test. Now, if you get mad, turn the television off, and say, "I'm not watching my show anymore!" you'd miss your show. What you don't realize is, it was just a test. Even if it wasn't a test, your instructions would have followed.

Similarly, when we look at the circumstances we are going through, it is God who has to create a situation for revelation. I need to recognize that the problem I'm in, the struggle I'm having, where I am at the moment, what I'm going through, this is merely a test. It is a moment in which I get to meet God and get pulled out of my comfort zone. It's a moment in which I get to experience God and get to move beyond my limitations. It is a moment where I get to wrestle with God and He pulls me into the next place. He has to create a situation for my revelation so that when my revelation expands, I am now moving into the next level. This is only a test; I will not stay in this problem! I am moving to the next level! I can't stop here because this is a test! This is a situation for my revelation!

God said, "Don't get the Esau syndrome. In other words, don't dumb My solution down to your problem. My solution is always higher than your problem." So if you're hungry, trust in the blessing that will produce the food. In context it's like this: If Esau would have said, "Wait a minute, I'm blessed!" I believe God would have made somebody walk by and hand him some food. But because he didn't value the blessing on his life, he sold it for some stew. He solved his problem, but he traded a lifelong gift for a short-term situation.

Some of you need to stand up and say, "Satan, this is not a lifelong situation; this is a short-term situation. My life is not dictated by you. My life is orchestrated by God."

That means time is no longer my issue and I have been liberated from time. So no matter how long you keep me pressed in, I am going to press in further because of my belief and faith in God. Jesus died for me so that the blessing of Abraham might come upon me which makes ma a partaker in the promise. Because I have a promise, I don't care what I have to go through. I don't care the struggle that I have. I don't care the fight that I'm in. I don't care what you throw at me because if I know that I'm saved, if I know that the blessing is on my life, if I know that I'm qualified, then I do it because God is with me! I go because God's got me! I'm sure because God is here!

I do not need anything but the situation and I'm thankful in the situation. This is why the apostle Paul said, "I glory in tribulation, knowing that what's working in me, I get to bring to you because the more I go through, the more revelation I'll walk in. The more revelation I walk in, the more I can help you. For this cause I bow my knees and I pray that you don't take what I go through as a bad thing. To walk in much revelation means I have to walk in much fight."

There's always resistance. You have everything you need because it's according to what worketh in you. You have to be careful that you don't let the situation talk you out of your blessing. What you'll do is proclaim your blessing over and over, and then when a problem happens, you'll rethink your blessing and think it's not real. At that moment, good luck. You'll need it. I'm talking to the person who wasn't qualified but got the job anyway. I'm talking to the person who just literally should have been dead. People you grew up with are dead. People in your family are gone. Things that took them out didn't take you out. Mama and others had such-and-such disease and died of it. Grandmama died of it. It runs in the family, but it hasn't come nigh you. I'm talking about where you begin to recognize it's not about luck. It's about His provision.

There are some things in your life you should've gone through. You were smoking it right next to them when they were doing it. You were running when they were running. You were robbing folks when they were robbing folks. You were out acting a fool when they were out acting a fool. But somehow what came to them didn't come to you. You slept with it and it had some issues but it didn't come to you. You went through some problems, and it didn't come to you.

I'm talking to real people. You've been through some real stuff where you know that you've had to see the provision of God. It wasn't luck; it was the provision of God. I had an experience with God and when I came out the other end, I had revelation of who He was and is and will forever be!

You weren't supposed to be here right now, but you are. You weren't supposed to be alive, but you are. When you flip through the hallmark of your mind and begin to reflect back on so-and-so who didn't make it, so-and-so who isn't here today, you develop a gratefulness. I might not be all that I want to be. I might not have all that I want to have, but I tell you what: I'm so glad for the situation that I'm in right now because this situation was created for my revelation. It is to help me to move beyond and see what I cannot see now; the mystery that's about to be revealed.

God is not one you can find. He has to be revealed and it is in His time and in His season that He allows you to see a glimpse of Him. Jacob walked away from wrestling with the angel and said, "I have seen the face of God." He didn't see the face of God, he saw what God was willing to reveal to him! No man has seen the face of God, but it was enough that what he saw, he said, "I saw the face of God! I wrestled and I won!"

What are you going to do when you have to wrestle for your victory? What are you going to do when you have to fight for your victory? I'm talking about going after this thing, recognizing it's not just going to fall into your lap. Some of the situations you're going through are for your revelation. You're wondering why you keep going through it over and over again. Check your revelation.

As your revelation goes to the next level, so do you. If I want God to be large in what I see, then He has to be large in me. So now all of a sudden when I'm in the situation, when the Bible says that I glory in tribulations, when the Bible says in James that I will fall into divers temptations, I know that the trying of my faith works patience. I need to let patience have its perfect work. In other words, don't be too hasty to get out of the situation you're in because if the situation is for your revelation, then staying in the situation is what brings revelation.

So therefore I glory in my tribulations. I thank God for this problem He's given me because it's working in me a far more eternal weight of glory! When I come out of this thing, I'm going to come out not even smelling like smoke. I'm going to come out better. I'm going to be sharper. I'm going to be wiser. I'm going to be more gifted. I'm going to be more anointed. I'm going to be more talented! When I come out, I'm coming out with a new revelation and watch out! When I come out with a new revelation, it's on like Donkey-Kong now. Another problem will come, another situation will come, but I'm blessed. And when I'm blessed, I'm too blessed to be stressed. I'm too anointed to be disappointed.

When David ran to the battle, he ran not because he was afraid, and not because he trusted in himself. The first thing he said was, "The battle is not mine, it is the LORD's." When you begin to understand what the battle is working in you, you become settled. I have to go through this. I'm not trying to get out of this. I'm not trying to get a solution real quick. I want the revelation of who God is. If I have to wrestle with Him, I might come out with a limp, but I'm going to wrestle until I get it. I'm going to wrestle until I come through it because I know that my God is well able to do exceedingly, abundantly more than I can ask or think according to the power that worketh in me. And I'm not willing to trade it just to get out of a short-term situation.

The blessing will work if you work it. I hear many people say, "Pastor, I can't afford to do this. I'm on a fixed income." Who fixed it? You know who fixed it? You, because you keep saying it. I told you that I get care packages every day. I can't wait to see what comes in the mail; something's coming! You want to know why? I expect it. I confess it. I believe it. Therefore, I get it. Every situation I have to go through is a situation created for my revelation because I now have come to the understanding that when He said, *"Who you say that I am* is now affected by My relationship with you. Who do they say that I am? They are not close to Me like you." He asked, "Who do they say that I am?" because they were not a part of the three that were the closest to Him. The closest to Jesus are the ones who go through the greatest attack. The revelation of who He is to you will be formed in the attack. It is formed and rooted in proximity. The closer you are to Jesus, the better the picture is you have of Him.

I love all of you, so please don't take this the wrong way. But a lot of people say things like, "Pastor, I love you." You don't love me, you love "Pastor" because you don't even know me. You don't know anything about me really, or you may know a little. My wife can love me because she knows me. Her proximity gives her information that you don't have. So now if I say to her, "Who do you say that I am?" her answer is different than when I say to one of you, "Who do you say that I am?" So the closer you get to the revelation of who God really is, who He says He is, would mean that you have to increase your proximity and have to increase your encounters with Him. If I want you to become closer to me, I would have to have more dates with you. And in order for us to have a date, I'd have to put you into a situation that proves you need a date that'll meet you at the restaurant. So when I show up, you are waiting for me and you are ready to have this encounter coming out of the situation that was created for your revelation. In every situation, I get to reveal myself to you.

They Hate Us 'Cause They Ain't Us

Genesis 26:12-22; 26:32-33

"Then Isaac sowed in that land, and received in the same year an hundredfold: and the LORD blessed him. And the man waxed great, and went forward, and grew until he became very great; For he had possession of flocks, and possession of herds, and great store of servants: and the Philistines envied him. For all the wells which his father's servants had digged in the days of Abraham his father, the Philistines had stopped them, and filled them with earth. And Abimelech said unto Isaac, Go from us; for thou art much mightier than we. And Isaac departed from there, and pitched his tent in the valley of Gerar, and dwelt there. And Isaac digged again the wells of water, which they had digged in the days of Abraham, his father; for the Philistines had stopped them after the death of Abraham: and he called their names after the names by which his father had called them. And Isaac's servants digged in the valley, and found there a well of springing water. And the herdsmen of Gerar did strive with Isaac's herdsmen, saying, The water is ours: and he called the name of the well Esek; because they strove with him. And they digged another well, and strove for that also: and he called the name of it Sitnah. And he removed from there, and digged another well; and for that they strove not: and he called the name of it Rehoboth; and he said, For now the LORD hath made room for us, and we shall be fruitful in the land....And it came to pass the same day, that Isaac's servants came, and told him concerning the well which they had digged, and said unto him, We have found water. And he called it Shebah: therefore the name of the city is Beersheba unto this day."

149

Here, Isaac is beginning to reap what has been promised to his father. He enters into a land and the Bible says he sowed in that land.

It's interesting to read that even though there's a great famine in the land, Isaac began to sow and the Bible says that he reaped a hundredfold harvest. A hundredfold doesn't necessarily mean a hundred times, it means the fullness of that which was planted. So you have to recognize that while your crop is determined by your seed, your harvest is determined by the ground. When I plant, if I plant apples, I don't expect to get oranges. If I plant an apple tree, I'll get an apple tree. The type of seed that I plant will certainly determine the type of harvest I have, but the quantity of apples on that tree will depend on the soil I planted it in.

That helps me to understand that it is not necessarily a requirement of mine to begin to determine how increase comes, but to make sure that I'm good soil for the increase. The Bible says that Paul planted and Apollos watered but God brought the increase. We know that increase comes by virtue of God's blessing upon our lives. As God's blessing is on our lives, then increase has to come. It says some thirty, some sixty, some a hundredfold. That means that people, things, and situations can produce in relative terms—not necessarily relative to your faith, although faith is an important ingredient—but that God is the One who brings increase into a situation.

When Isaac came into the land and that land was in famine, God didn't tell him to leave. He said, "Yes, they're in famine. Yes, it's in recession. Yes, there are economic challenges, yes the climate is struggling. Yes they're hard to deal with, but you have to sow in that land because if you sow in any other land, then the increase I will bring will not demonstrate My power. I need you to sow in that land."

So many people are looking for new land. They're waiting for God to move them on to something bigger. "If You just give me a new job,

God; if You would just give me a new house; God, if You would just give me a new spouse; God, if You'd just give me..."

Isaac sowed in *that* land, in a land where everyone else was experiencing famine in the midst of a recession, losing their homes, losing their jobs, struggling. When you turn on the news, it's nothing but doom and gloom. So many people want to sit back and say, "Let's pray that all of this changes. These people don't like us so they're coming after us to kill us. This group of people doesn't want Christianity to be proclaimed. This group of people wants us dead. Do you realize that all these things are happening in the world?" Yeah, I get all that, BUT MY GOD SAID that if I sow in that land, the difference between me and them is Him.

He plants and he sows in a land that's hostile. He begins to do what others have been doing with no result. Some thirty, some sixty, but he reaped a hundredfold. Anybody can tell you how many seeds are in the apple, but only God can tell you how many apples are in the seed. You have to understand that he sowed in *that* land and in that land he reaped a full harvest.

This flies in the face of the idea that climate and economic situations and circumstances all have to be right in order for me to prosper. Which then means that my prosperity is not a work of natural things, but it has to be a work of the spirit. If everyone else is struggling, then in order for me to prosper while others struggle, I have to have something that is more super than their natural. If it was all natural, Isaac would have sowed in that land and reaped the same results the others did. But, somehow, something must have moved beyond the norm, beyond the natural, and took him into a place of abundance. It had to be his father who had received a promise. Not only was it promised to Abraham, but it was promised to all of his generations.

If you read the entire text, you will find God reminds him that He swore an oath and a promise to Isaac's father, and this will help you in your situation. The moment that famine is announced, God tells Isaac to stay in this land. Now Isaac is dealing with the king and the first thing he does is, he lies to the king. They ask him, "This woman, is she your sister or your wife?" He says, "That's my sister." It was his wife. He flat-out lies. Here's one of those sacred cows we're about to barbecue right about now. So many of you have the impression that your behavior has to earn what God will do for you.

Joe Paterno was the head coach of the Penn State Nittany Lions and was the most winningest coach in Division I college football. He died not too long ago, two months after he was fired for a scandal that broke out at Penn State. He was not the aggressor nor the victim, yet he was fired. They took down his statue that was erected in his honor.

It is interesting to me because the very nature of legacy makes us wonder what it is that people will think about you when you're gone. Here, this man had a statue erected in his honor for being the winningest coach, the top, the creme de la creme, and his statue was taken down for his character. The statue was never erected because of his character, it was erected because he was the winningest coach. Therefore, because of his achievements they erected a statue but because of his character they tore it down. People do not recognize that the gift and the person are not always the same thing. My ability to win games may not be indicative of my character, but when people begin to idolize, they assume that because you're good at one thing, you're a good person.

Now enters Bill Cosby. Before all of the allegations began to transpire, he was given honorary degrees, and then people started taking them back. Now a whole man's legacy has been ruined. All that he did right in his life is now overshadowed by what he did wrong. Whether he did it or not, it is bizarre to me that my lowest level of listening is to factor the messenger instead of the message. The truth of the matter is, one can do great things and still struggle. A person can have great exploits and still have problems.

When the Bible says Abraham is the father of the faith, that does not imply that he was a man who had complete and utter faith as much as the fact that he was faithful. To be full of faith and faithful are two very different things. Apparently, Isaac felt the need to lie as he said, "The reason I lied to you, king, is because I thought you would kill me because my wife is fine. So I figured since she's fine and you're asking questions, I'll go ahead and say she's my sister." That shows you he was not full of faith. If he was full of faith, we assume he would stand back and say, "My God is well able!" But he didn't. It just so happened that the king was looking out his window and saw them sporting together and he said, "What is this you've done to us? Why would you lie?" So it's possible that the gift and the person could very well be separated in its manifestation.

I'm not proposing or suggesting that you lie. I'm not even endorsing the idea of evil. Just because you may have done some things, that does not change whether or not you are blessed. One of the things people begin to think is, "Well, if I hadn't done this and that and, man, I wish I hadn't done..." There may be consequences to your actions in the natural, but that does not negate the blessing as the blessing is us-ward.

If God is a man who cannot lie, then whatever He has promised when He swore by an oath and made a covenant, it is not based on your dependability. It is not based on your consistency. It is not based on your trustworthiness. It is based on Him; He who has decreed a thing; He who is the one who spoke that; He who is the one who is the conferrer of all blessing! It is based on His personality, trustability, and Him alone. So then my ability to be see myself through the lens of God now will change my interpretation of my life. When I see myself through myself, I begin to skew because I condemn. Nobody is harder on you than you. You may not say anything, but in the stillness and quietness of your own mind, nobody will beat you up like you beat yourself up.

We see that Isaac planted four wells. The first well that he planted he called "strife." The first stage of the manifestations of blessings in your life will always be strife. I don't mean strife in your home or your heart. I don't mean strife in your world. I mean the world hates you. They hate us because they ain't us. Anytime the manifestations of the blessing come into your life, the first thing you will find is strife with them. Who is "*them*"? Those who are without. You can lose sight of what is supposed to happen because you'll get lost in the strife. It will come because they're not going to just turn it over. This is why Isaac named the first one strife. He says, "The first thing I'm going to encounter is some level of resistance."

If you are facing Satan, you're going to run into him head-on at some point in time. If you think that somehow you have been granted a life that is devoid of problems, challenges, and issues, if you think that you can just believe God and no problems come, everything will be perfect, and you are benchmarking your life based on perfection of what you deem it to be, you are in La-La Land. The Bible says *many* are the afflictions of the righteous, but my God delivers them out of them all. This means that the presence of God in my life and the favor of God on my life does not diminish the attacks to my life. What it actually does is, it gives me solutions when I have no hope. Thus, the presence of strife is a clear indication that I have entered into the first stage. But if I give up in the first stage, I'll never make it to the second.

The Bible says that others envied Isaac. There's a difference between envy and jealousy; envy is when two parties have a problem. One party has something specific that the second party would like to have and doesn't. I could look at somebody and say, "Wow, you have a really nice car!" And I can move into envy because they have something that I do not have. That is not jealousy. I don't have the car; it doesn't belong to me. Jealousy would kick in when they offer to give my wife a ride in it and not me. They envied Isaac, yet they were in the same place; they had the same things. They had the same jobs, they worked in the same company, they lived in the same town, they were with him in the same place. They had what he had, but they were not jealous, they were envious. What he had, they didn't have and they wanted it.

The second well was named "Sidna" which means hatred. When we move out of strife and God gives us the victory, they're going to hate us because they ain't us. The development of strife always moves into hatred because you have it and they don't. You overcame and they didn't. This is a problem especially in cultures of people who have slightly more melanin in their skin than others, of which I'm an authority. As you begin to grow beyond the confines of what is imposed by family, they hate us because they ain't us. "Why do you always have to go to that church? Why do you always have to spend so much time there?" (If you were in the club there'd be no discussion.) "Why do you think you have to go to school and get a degree? None of us did. You just think you're better than us."

If you give in to that, you'll end up in the same socioeconomic situation they are, then you'll be wishing and saying, "I could've been a contender; I could've been somebody." But if I allow you to pull my heartstrings, you will pull me right back into the strife and cause me to never get to the next level. They hate us 'cause they ain't us.

When you move into, "I'm ignoring your strife, all of your comments about, 'Why do you have to do this? Why do you think you're better than us? You just think you're special. You movin' out of the hood. You movin' up and got a better car and a better house and a better this and a better life. You gettin' married...' " Listen, don't take marriage advice from your single friends. Trust me when I tell you, your girlfriend does not want you to get married. She wants you to stay busted and disgusted like her so you have something to talk about.

Most people struggle with the dynamic of a relationship—not because they don't want you to be better, it's because they don't want the relationship to change. You have to be very careful because *they* come in many different forms. Once you can get past the strife, then they hate you. That's when you show up at the house and they're talking about you. "I hate them!" "Why? What'd they do?" "They just think they're better than us!" They hate us. Now all of a sudden they have progressed beyond the strife because once they learned they can't strive with you anymore, the strife immediately progresses to hatred.

The third well Isaac built was called "Rahobeth" which means "room or space." Space is a place of enlarging, a place where I flourish. When I begin to flourish, that means I begin to expand in ways that are different than you. I have to get past the strife. I have to make it through the hatred. When I don't care anymore how you feel about me, I've made it.

So many people are so concerned about what other people think and say about them. There are things about you that the world will hate and they hate it, just because you're you. You haven't done anything. It is the understanding that something is different about you. "I'm not quite sure what it is, but I don't like them. I don't like them because when I had to go through this layoff, I didn't have a job for months. Here, so-and-so gets laid off and the next day they get a job. I make what so-and-so makes, but somehow they always have and I don't. I don't understand why it is that God loves them more than he loves me." This is how people think. This becomes the genesis of their strife and hatred. The truth of the matter is, they hate us 'cause they ain't us. It's not a measure of jealousy because they don't have what we have. It's a measure of envy—both of which are detrimental to a relationship, but you need to understand why.

Jealousy requires three things. Envy is when you don't like what I have. Jealousy now moves between you and me and now there's a third something that you want or believe is threatened by my presence. Hence, the analogy of the car. If you have a nice car, that's great! I can be envious because you have a nice car, but if you offer to give my wife a ride, what makes me jealous is not the car, it's my wife. When the Bible says others envy you, that builds hatred in them.

The question I have to ask is, if they're all in the same place, you mean to tell me that Joe and I can work at the same plant, Joe can get fired and I can get fired, but I can expect to be blessed and Joe doesn't? Is that a measure of my faith, or is it a measure of the blessing? We understand that we've been redeemed from the curse of the law so that the blessing of Abraham might come upon the Gentiles. We become heirs according to the promise. If Joe and I can be in the same company and Joe's not a believer, but I am, is it a measure of my faith that will produce better than him or is it a measure of the blessing that's on my life? If the blessing is not dependent upon me, but it is what it is, then the only reason why they would hate us and envy us is if we had something they didn't.

Let's take a look at the story of Joe Paterno again. If by implication I can bestow something upon him based on his achievements and not have any indication of his character, then that means I don't always have the ability to discern what he did or didn't do in the realm of his character. I'm blessing him according to what I decided to do for him based on him. This means if that's why I gave it to him, I don't take it back. Now, if the statue was erected because he was a man of great character, or we found out that he cheated in all 409 games that he won, then I would take the statue back because of the very nature of why I gave it to him.

So then if I'm blessed, then I'm blessed. If the reason I gave it to you had nothing to do with your character, then I am not unrighteous enough to take back from you what I gave to you. It had nothing to do with you, but had everything to do with me. So when I bestow it upon you, it is so that Joe—who's sitting next to you—can see in you what is different in you that he does not have.

So then it is quite possible that in the plan of God, envy is necessary. There has got to be something different about you. I'm not trying to create jealousy in my family. Jealousy is when you both have it, but you think my relationship's different. If I'm blessed, if I'm a child of God, then so are you. If there's anything I have that you have a problem with, you moved into jealousy because you have the same blessing. Thus, the implication is that the relationship I have with Him is somehow different. The people who become envious are the ones who are without because they do not have what you have. They cannot do what you are able to do. They are going through the exact same situations in life that you are. They are digging the exact same wells the same way you are. They are living in the exact same places you do. They are in the same type of houses you are.

It's hard for me to believe that God would want people to be envious of us, but they have to be. The only way the perceived difference exists is if it is, in fact, perceived. If I looked at you and you are no different than me, if every time you go through a problem and I go through a problem we respond the exact same way, if we're sitting around the water cooler together talking about how the company is laying off people and you say, "I sure hope they don't take my job!" then you and I are exactly the same. This means you have what I have and I have what you have. There is no need for me to be envious. We will both end up in the same pot.

The only way envy comes in is if I'm sitting around the water cooler with you and I say, "I can't believe they are laying folks off!" And you say, "I couldn't care less, because this job is not my source." My source is Almighty God, and unless you're telling me that they fired Him, then we have nothing to talk about because He will move me from one place to the next. He will promote me from one job to the next. He will take care of me from one situation to the next because if I move from faith to faith and from glory to glory and from victory to victory, then I am assured that my God is well able! So now there is absolutely no need for me to be envious of you, but, in fact, we now have the basis of envy towards me.

There's a business principle called The Methuselah Theory, which is the idea that just because you've been there the longest, you're the one who gets promoted. That's not true. The reason they call it The Methuselah Theory is because Methuselah is the oldest person recorded in the Bible. When I move past the strife (because strife is my first stage and there's always that struggle that people are not going to allow you to be blessed) they're going to fight that. It's always when you're trying to save up for something that somebody wants to come and borrow something. It's working contrary to you. It's designed to keep you out of what God is trying to take you in.

Most people give up in the strife stage. If you happen to make it past the strife, then you move into, "I just can't tolerate the fact that they don't like me. They have to like me. What if they don't like me anymore? What if my mama doesn't like me anymore? What if my friends don't like me anymore? What if my dad doesn't like me anymore? What if my best friend doesn't like me anymore? You understand I can pay my bills with their like!" So we become victims of what *like* brings, not realizing that the envy is necessary. We get swooned over whether they like us. Will they be mad at us? What will they tell the family? What will they tell the rest of them? What stories will they make up?

If I am successful enough to get to the place where I don't care anymore, then I move into "Rahobeth", or making room. So many of us want to see the big blessing before we go through the strife and the hatred. God said you don't get it that way. You have to endure the situation you're in. He needs you to get through that and not be moved by how people think and see you. When He makes room for you, when He begins to enlarge you, He can't have them directing you. You're going to have to direct them because you can't help them in the situation until He makes room for you.

Some people will be mad today and you're going to have to endure it so that tomorrow you can reach back and say, "I know you're mad, but I have arrived. Now I can bless you because I'm blessed to be a blessing. You can stay mad all you want, but I can help now because I've been enlarged."

God said if He's going to bless you, He can't have you led by your emotions. Isaac was great, then he became very great. You can't be very great and be manipulated by your kids. You can't be very great and be manipulated by your lover. You can't be very great and be manipulated by your family. If you want to be very great, the only One who's going to "manipulate" you is God Himself. He says what He needs from you is not to be full of faith, but to be faithful. Faithful means I'll go when He tells me to go, I'll stop when He tells me to stop. I'll walk when He tells me to walk, and I'll do it the way He's asked me to do it. Not that I'm full of faith; I am faithful. I'll take a step when He tells me to take that step. So now it becomes an indication of my faithfulness and not necessarily my faith. If I want the enlarging, I have to learn how to overcome strife.

The last well Isaac called "Sheba," which stands for "promise." I go through this struggle and I know they're going to hate me and I move into where God starts to enlarge me. Isaac named the well "Sheba" because now all of his enemies had begun to depend on him. All of those around him were now at peace with him. The promise didn't start in the beginning. What God promised to Abraham is now in full manifestation.

The fourth stage is where it becomes evident that I'm walking in the blessing. You see somebody with a new house and you say, "Oh, that is such a blessing." You see somebody with a new car and you say, "Oh, that is such a blessing!" That is not a blessing, that's a manifestation of the blessing. The blessing is on you, and if you are blessed, you will manifest if you endure. But so many are willing to give up and they're running around wondering why they don't see the promise. They're a joint heir to the promise, but they don't see the promise.

Similarly, you can't see the promise because you're still in the strife. You can't see the promise because you're too worried about who hates you. You can't see the promise because God is ready to make room for you. You're in stages of this thing and you have to recognize where you are. If you think you're going to see it from jump, you will not. It's a process by which God takes you through first to deal with you, second to deal with your circumstance, then third to let people know that the God of Abraham, Isaac, and Jacob is the same God you serve! If you don't know who He is, let me help you to understand; they hate us because they ain't us!

What do we have that they don't? What do we manifest that they can't? And all the while it's easy. You could just turn to them and say, "If you will follow the same path, let me introduce you to my God. You no longer have to be jealous or envious." Jealousy usually comes from people who have the promise but don't walk in it. That's where you can sit with your sanctified self in the church and have people who are supposed to be your biggest fans, who should be your greatest encouragers, and they are hatin' on you.

Here's something I believe: haters are the breakfast of champions. If you don't hate on me, I'm not doing something right. If somebody isn't talking about me, I'm not doing this thing right. There has got to be that place where you understand that there are seasons to all of this. There's a process to all of this. But when it comes out in the wash, some will have thirty, some sixty, and some a hundredfold. It's not according to the seed because I'm sowing the right seeds. It's not according to the ground because I planted in the right ground. So it has to be God who giveth the increase. It might not be fair that I can have a farm right next to Joe's and mine produces a hundredfold at full capacity and his doesn't. It might not be fair that I work in the same place as so-and-so and we make the exact same amount of money, but I have more than they do. It might not be fair that so-and-so lost their job and I didn't. It might not be fair that I went through a situation and came out well and they didn't. It might not be fair that it killed them but it didn't kill me. It might not be fair that you succumbed to that situation but I didn't.

Now what I'm clear on is that you and I could be in the same place, in the same economy, work at the same job, but because the blessing's on me, I'm going to be all right. You just keep on with your hatin' self because I've come to the realization of a truth: they hate us because they ain't us.

It's a sad state of affairs when other people know you're blessed more than you do. I've seen people who have gone through things and I've watched God move. I'm talking about people who have had to go through a divorce and God brought them through it; others who were wrecked and destroyed and God brought them through. I'm talking about those people who had to fight with sickness in their body to the point of death but God brought them through while other people died. I'm talking about those people who got strung out in their addictions and their pipe partner is dead and they're not. I'm talking about those people who went through economic situations. They didn't have money and struggled but they are climbing out, while the person who struggled with them is still struggling. I'm talking about people who have been in the same situation with the same struggles and the same problems as others, yet God has delivered them. Your God has shown Himself faithful. Your God has shown Himself strong. Your God has shown up and shown out. Your God wouldn't let you fall. Your God wouldn't let you fail. You watched other people in the same situation and you're like, "I don't know what's wrong. Why are you mad at me that I came out and you didn't?" It's the blessing.

Paul said, "When I come to the end of myself I glory in tribulations. I understand when I come through persecutions. I have struggles and problems; it's going to happen. But when I come to myself, when I come to the end of me, then in that place is where my God steps in" (see Romans 5:3). You have to understand that's why he was saying, "I can count myself a Pharisee. By intellectual standards,

I'm smart. But I count all of that as dung. What I know is the God who moveth in me, who causes me to do and the will of His good pleasure. It is not of myself, it is of my God" (see Philippians 3:8). Now we begin to see this in manifestation. It is not until you increase in your revelation that God makes room. You want God to enlarge you in the strife? You can't get enlarged in the strife because the enemy might take it. It's only when you come out of that and you don't care anymore that you get the victory.

Now God says, "Okay, now I'm going to enlarge you. Now I'm going to expand you. Now I'm going to take you to Rahobeth and make room for you. Now I'm able to do some things because you don't care what mama and them think. You ain't manipulated by your friends and them. Now I have the ability to move in your life the way I want to. Now you can have that hundredfold. Now you can reap what others can't reap. Now when you sow, it produces full. Now when you do something, it works. Now when you buy that business, it booms. It might've failed in their hands, but when it got into yours... That car might not have worked well in someone else's hands, that's why they sold it so cheap, but all of a sudden, when it got into your hands... He might not have loved her like you were going to love her, so he had to treat her wrong to get her to understand and be ready for you. So you stepped into her life and now all of a sudden, she's ready for you because of him." There were things God had to do. It wasn't right for him, but it's now right for you.

Some of you judge books by their covers and don't even know God is working.

You look at the business that's not doing well and say, "Who would buy a business that ain't doing well?" If God told you to buy it, buy it. If He told you to do it, you'd better do it. He might not be Mr. Right Now but he might be Mr. Right. If God told you, you better do it. This is how God works. The enlarging doesn't happen until you get past you. You might meet him today and he might drive the bus, but you have no idea the plan of God for his life.

Any idiot can tell you how many seeds are in the apple, but only God can tell you how many apples are in a seed. You're too busy getting stuck at what you see on the outside, not realizing that when it comes into your life, it has to produce, even though it might not have produced for them. They might have dug 800 wells, holes all around the place, but God will lead you to the right spot and say, "Right there." If you are faithful, God will put you in the right place at the right time. You might be sitting at the water cooler talking about how nobody gets promoted. Really? Get away from that water cooler, go back to your desk, and do your job and watch God take care of the situation! Nobody else will get promoted; you'll get promoted! That's the blessing that's on my life.

The gospel is the good news. It's not good news to tell me that I have to suffer like you suffer. That is not good news! Good news is when you tell me that what you have to deal with, I might have to go there for a little bit, but I have answers. Now that tells me that blessing and curse could be in the same room but not on the same people. I could be sitting at my desk closing deals and you're sitting across from me and you're not. I could be sitting at my desk and get a phone call that says, "We need to talk to you about a new position, a new promotion." And the lady across from you who's been there ten times longer than you will still be sitting at the water cooler talking about how nobody gets promoted. This implies that I can be in the same place as you, I could be in the same situation as you, yet I'll walk away with totally different results.

It's like this. Let's say a minister decides that God puts it on their heart that they should get a private jet. Do I think there are extremes? I do. We just got back from Houston; I wouldn't want to live in Houston. No offense to Houston. If you live in Houston, please understand I love you, but I couldn't live there. Through the traveling experience you kind of understand some things. It takes about 18 hours to get from here to Houston. We got up at 3 a.m., but didn't get to our destination until 3 p.m. on commercial airlines. Standing in line for this and that; put your clothes on, take your clothes off. They don't even buy you dinner, no flowers, no nothing. We had to fly to Houston, rent a car, drive two hours to our destination, and there was an airport to where we were going, but it wasn't a commercial airport. However, when you fly privately, you can fly directly to that city, which means I wouldn't have had to rent a car and drive two hours.

I began to process some of these things and think, I understand now about people who have to travel a lot; but I never heard anybody argue about the CEO of American Express and the jet he flies in. I've never heard Christians complain on social media about the CEO of Coca-Cola (the CEO who sells sugar water) saying "Can you believe he spent $25 million dollars!" I began to realize something. Envy and jealousy are not the same thing. The world is not envious of its own because they have what they have. Therefore, there's nothing to post about because it's of itself. The only people who tend to say those negative things are those who are jealous. Not because he has something they don't have, but somehow they feel their relationship with God changes.

I started to think, "What do we have to be jealous of?" Here's what I've learned. You have no idea what we have to do in order to preach the gospel. This building is wonderful, but there was a time when I had to preach in a 20'x20' room in the upstairs of my house with five people. I love this building, I love where we came from and where we're going. But you have no idea what it was like to have to believe God for stuff when you didn't have people sharing the load. You don't know what it was like for me to have to have a yard sale to sell my stuff in order to put food on my table, yet show up and preach and talk about how great God is. I had to bring spiritual food to you, yet, I didn't have natural food on my own table. That's why I don't judge what another man does, because what you don't know is the strife and the hatred they had to endure.

Now that means that when I get involved with you, it depends on what stage you're at and how much I know about it. If I get around you when God is making room for you, I didn't see the strife you might've had to endure. I don't know the price you've had to pay. All I see is now you might be flying around, but I had no idea when you had to sleep in the pew of your own church because you didn't have a house. I didn't see when you didn't have food on your own table.

Once you start getting jealous, you'd better be careful what you see because you might see a person in the stage of being enlarged, not realizing the price they had to pay to get there. I can't be mad at you because you're willing to pay a price I was afraid to pay! We might have started a business at the same time, but when things got tough you might have bailed and got a "real job". So now that you see the business has grown and now I'm enjoying the benefits of my room being expanded, don't you hate on me because I made it! Don't you hate on me because I've taken the next step! Don't you hate on me because God is enlarging! That's why I have nothing to say about the prosperity of anybody else in ministry. I don't know the price they had to pay.

I remember one time T.D. Jakes said, "I had one suit and I had to wash it in the washing machine and iron it." If you know anything about suits, you do not put a suit in the washer and you definitely don't dry it. He said, "I used to not want to kneel down and pray because I had holes in the soles of my shoes that I had placed cardboard in."

You don't know the struggle that other people had to endure to get where they are. Be careful that you don't see people in their enlarging phase where God starts to increase them, because there will be no increase without the struggle. If you don't want to go through the struggle, can I have it?

What I've learned is, I will never be increased without the struggle. God is always creating the situation for my revelation. Some of you thought the struggle was a sign that you did something wrong. You didn't do anything 'wrong, you're on your way. They hate us 'cause they ain't us.

www.ingramcontent.com/pod-product-compliance
Lightning Source LLC
LaVergne TN
LVHW051059080426
835508LV00019B/1963